RESTLESS SPIRIT

By the Author

THE LIVES AND TIMES OF PETER COOPER

RESTLESS SPIRIT: THE LIFE OF EDNA ST. VINCENT
MILLAY

RESTLESS SPIRIT

The Life of Edna St. Vincent Millay

MIRIAM GURKO

Thomas Y. Crowell Company · New York

B

Acknowledgments

Acknowledgment is made to Norma Millay Ellis for permission to quote the poems or fragments of poems and letters in this book, from the following sources, all published by Harper & Brothers: *Collected Poems*, copyright 1912, 1917, 1918, 1919, 1920, 1921, 1922, 1923, 1928, 1931, 1933, 1934, 1936, 1937, 1938, 1939, 1940, 1941, 1945, 1946, 1947, 1950 by Edna St. Vincent Millay; copyright 1945, 1946, 1947, 1948, 1950, 1951, 1952, 1953, 1954, 1955, 1956, 1958 by Norma Millay Ellis. *The King's Henchman*, copyright 1927 by Edna St. Vincent Millay; copyright 1954 by Norma Millay Ellis. *Aria da Capo*, copyright 1920, 1947 by Edna St. Vincent Millay. *Make Bright the Arrows*, copyright 1940 by Edna St. Vincent Millay. *Distressing Dia-*

To Floyd Dell

Foreword

THE material for this book was drawn from a wide range of sources which included memoirs, articles, doctoral dissertations, the Millay collection at the Vassar library, the writings and interviews of Edna St. Vincent Millay herself, and personal interviews and correspondence with people who had known her during her lifetime. Curiously, as the mass of notes grew, the more elusive the subject seemed to become. Every person presents a different image at different periods of his life and to different people at any time, but Edna Millay's image varied so widely and often so inconsistently that it hardly seemed possible in a series of interviews, for example, that the same person was being discussed. Even specific incidents would be presented with greatly varying and at times contradictory details.

From this assortment of fact and characterization I have had to select those elements which appeared the most credible, and which seemed to have undergone the least alteration as a result of the passage of time or the presence of special personal factors. Whenever possible, I have used the version which had the greatest documentary support. I am aware, however, that among those who knew Edna Millay personally, there might be some who will disagree with my portrayal of her. They will say that this is not *their* Edna. They may be entirely right. It was not my intention to present any one person's Edna any more than it was to include every known detail of her life. My aim has been to set down the most pertinent facts and to try to throw some light on that volatile and extraordinary personality as it developed over the years. In addition, her poetry, her viewpoints and problems as a poet, and her place in her own lively period are among the principal themes of my book.

I have tried to be scrupulously accurate. If error has crept in, I can only repeat in my defense what Edna Millay said about an error of fact which she made while trying to convince Governor Fuller of Massachusetts of his possible error in the Sacco-Vanzetti case. She had told him the story of the last execution in the state of Maine as she remembered hearing it in her childhood. The account turned out to be wrong, and some of the many people who hastened to correct her were in their turn proved wrong. In a letter to the New York *World* unraveling this chain of errors, she wrote: "As an illustration of the fallibility of the human mind I told him the story as I remembered it. . . . If in the very illustration which I used I was myself in error, the force of my assertion is not lessened—that human beings with the best intentions in the world often made mistakes."

In a book of this kind it is not possible to give immediate footnote acknowledgment of the sources for individual items, much as I would like to do so. Among the most valuable works providing direct information and from which excerpts, facts, or incidents have been used are *Homecoming* (Farrar & Rinehart) and "Not Roses, Roses All the Way" (unpublished) by Floyd Dell, "Epilogue, 1952: Edna St. Vincent Millay" in *The Shores of Light* by Edmund Wilson (Farrar, Straus and Young), *The Indigo Bunting* by Vincent Sheean (Harper), *Great Companions* by Max Eastman (Farrar, Straus and Cudahy), *The Improper Bohemians* by Allen Churchill (Dutton), "Mother of Poets" and "Edna St. Vincent Millay" by Elizabeth Breuer (*Pictorial Review*), "Husband of a Genius" by Allan Ross Macdougall (*Delineator*), "Vincent at Vassar" and "Vincent at Steepletop" by Elizabeth Hazelton Haight (*Vassar Alumnae Magazine*),

"Edna St. Vincent Millay's Youth" by Ethel Knight Fisher (*St. Nicholas Magazine*), " 'Best Sellers' in Verse, the Story of Edna St. Vincent Millay" by Jerome Beatty (*The American Magazine*), "The 'Vincent' Camden Knew" by Richard D. Estes (*Yankee*), and *The Development of the Social Consciousness of Edna St. Vincent Millay as Manifested in Her Poetry* by Grace Hamilton King (unpublished doctoral dissertation, New York University). *Letters of Edna St. Vincent Millay*, edited by Allan Ross Macdougall (Harper), was especially important, not only for the letters themselves but also for the biographical notes included in the volume. The descriptions of the judges' reading of "Renascence," and its first reading by Arthur Ficke and Witter Bynner, are taken from these notes. All the letters quoted, both in the epigraphs and in the text, are from this collection, with the exception of the two early letters (1917) to Charlotte Babcock Sills. All the poems, both in the epigraphs and text, are by Edna St. Vincent Millay, unless otherwise indicated. All her poetry and letters, from whatever source, are reprinted with the kind permission of Norma Millay Ellis (see copyright page).

I wish to extend my thanks and appreciation to the authors of the above works and of others too numerous to include here. A more complete and detailed listing will be found in the bibliography.

To all those who granted me interviews or engaged in correspondence with me, I wish to express my warm thanks. They are in no way responsible for the use I have made of any information they were kind enough to give me. My deepest appreciation must go to Norma Millay for her generosity in granting permission to quote extensively from the work of Edna Millay and for the great care and interest with which she brought errors in the text to my attention. My thanks go also to Charles Ellis, Robert Hunter Patterson, Joan Taylor, Frances Stout Kallman, Louise Bogan, Isobel Simpson Licht, Dante Bergonzi, Rosemary Benét, Abbie Huston Evans, Virginia Kirkus, Dr. Elaine Ralli, Esther Root Adams, Witter Bynner, Max Eastman, Henry Carter, Harriett Weiffenbach Long, Cecilia Vennard Sargent, Stella Derry Lenfest, Edith Smith Bailey, and to many others who cannot be listed individually but for whose interest and response I am grateful. Thanks are due also to Dorothy Plum of the Vassar College library for her patience and helpfulness, to the librarians at Vassar, Hunter, Yale, and other universities who assisted me in my research or allowed me to examine unpublished documents in their collections, and to the American Academy of Arts and Letters for letting me see the *Commemorative Tribute to Edna St. Vincent Millay* by Deems Taylor. Special thanks must go to Mrs. Charlotte Babcock Sills, who gave me unstinting access to her collection of Millay material and contributed significantly to my knowledge of the Vassar years.

Finally, I want to express my gratitude to Floyd Dell, who gave me such a largesse of information, suggestions, encouragement, and textual correction of the manuscript that he has infused with genuine meaning that form of dedication which states ". . . without whom this book could not have been written," and it is to him, therefore, that this book is dedicated.

Contents

xiii

RESTLESS SPIRIT

1.

Mr. and Mrs. Millay

"Meseems it never rained in those days."
          —*From* The King's Henchman.
    Quoted in a letter as descriptive of her childhood.

IN a letter written near the end of her life, Edna St. Vincent Millay said that her childhood had been "extraordinarily happy." There was little of the loneliness or misunderstanding which poets are traditionally supposed to endure in their early years. Instead, she flourished in the warmly expressed affection of a lively family, and was given an unusual degree of understanding and encouragement.

Some of the legends about Edna Millay have presented her as an example of urban sophistication; but she grew up in a series of small, simple New England towns, chiefly on the Maine seacoast, far removed from the complex worlds she was later to inhabit, both in reality and in the legends. She was born in Rockland, Maine, on February 22, 1892, a day thereafter celebrated by her family not as Washington's birthday, but as Edna St. Vincent Millay's. In apologizing for her failure to remember other people's birthdays, she was to say in later years that the only reason she ever remembered her own was that

1

it also happened to be observed as a national holiday.

The lilting, euphonious name was perfectly suited to the girl who would become one of America's greatest lyric poets. She never wanted to tell anyone how she got the curious name of "St. Vincent," but once, as a young woman, she gave this explanation: Not long before her birth, her mother's young sailor brother had been injured when his ship was caught in a violent storm. He was sent to St. Vincent's Hospital, where he received such good care that Mrs. Millay, as a way of expressing her gratitude, added the St. Vincent to her baby's name.

Her family and friends called her Vincent. It has been said that Mrs. Millay had expected a boy, and this was a possible reason for the emphasis on "Vincent" rather than "Edna." Whether or not the boyish name had anything to do with it, Vincent, growing up, did have more of the freedom ordinarily granted to boys rather than to girls.

She was the first child born to her parents, Henry Tolman and Cora Buzzelle Millay. After her birth, the Millays moved to Union, Maine, where Henry Millay became a high-school teacher and school superintendent. Two more girls were born, Norma in December, 1893, and Kathleen in May, 1896. Vincent had red hair, Norma was blonde, and Kathleen had dark brown hair.

Henry Millay, by all accounts, was a man with much charm but with an insufficient sense of family responsibility. He enjoyed gambling and sometimes his losses became too heavy for his family's comfort. Mr. and Mrs. Millay also differed in many of their ideas. There were various problems and the day came when Mrs. Millay had had enough. "I remember," wrote Edna Millay years later, "a swamp [of cranberries] . . . when I was seven. It was down across that swamp that my father went, when my mother told him to go & not come back.

"(Or maybe she said he might come back if he would do better—but who ever does better?)"

Her parents were divorced when Vincent was about eight. After their divorce Mr. and Mrs. Millay remained friends. Although he did not contribute regularly to their support, his daughters could ask him for anything special that they might want. He kept in touch with them and years later, when he became ill, Vincent went to stay with him. He was interested in the girls' careers and proud of their accomplishments. Nevertheless, the girls lacked a father in the ordinary domestic sense. From the time he left, the family really consisted of Cora Millay and her three lively daughters. The entire responsibility of bringing them up was now hers.

A broken home and economic insecurity hardly seem a foundation for an "extraordinarily happy" childhood. But the difficulties were confronted with an onslaught of energetic high spirits, and the deprivations were countered by warmth and mutual responsiveness. The absence of a father, however, couldn't be quite filled by either warmth or high spirits. It may even have shaped Vincent's later ideas about men and made her skeptical of the permanence of love, a theme that was to recur again and again in her poetry.

2.

Cora Millay

The courage that my mother had
Went with her, and is with her still:
Rock from New England quarried;
Now granite in a granite hill.

—Collected Poems.

CORA MILLAY was used to responsibility. Her mother had died early, leaving Cora with five younger sisters and brothers to help care for. Now she had undertaken to raise her own children entirely by her own efforts, and she set about it with vigor and determination.

She was as singular an individual, as independent and as forthright, as her eldest daughter was to become. She was unafraid of life, and met its problems with originality and grace. The 1890's were still haunted by a Victorian disapproval of divorce, and the economic opportunities open to women were meager. To divorce one's husband and voluntarily assume financial responsibility for a family required a formidable degree of courage. It needed even more than courage: it took a sure knowledge of her own worth, and the ability to choose a course of action and pursue it in the face of the social and economic pressures of the period.

She was talented as well as courageous. As a girl, she

4

had studied singing. While her daughters were growing up, she took an active part in the work of the town orchestra, writing out orchestral parts, playing the piano, and helping with rehearsals. Music formed an integral part of her children's background.

She read omnivorously and was at home in the world of literature. She had always wanted to write professionally and she contributed poems, short stories, and longer serialized pieces to several New England newspapers. She often sang her children to sleep and entertained them with songs and stories of her own composition.

Increasing cares both before and after marriage had made it impossible for her to realize her own professional ambitions. But the habit and need of expression had become so ingrained that whenever she had a scrap of time to spare, she would work at her writing. When her daughters were grown and she had more leisure, she published a book of verse for children called *Little Otis*.

It was her own frustration as a writer and musician, Mrs. Millay said later, that determined her to give her children the chance she had lacked. She set to work with almost missionary zeal to develop whatever talents they might possess. There was no hothouse forcing of "creative activities," but she provided them with enough background and experience in the arts to stimulate their own interests, and then encouraged whatever spark was aroused. She stirred their curiosity and created an atmosphere of active participation in art and literature. Whenever the girls came across a classical allusion, for example, she would respond to their question with "Look it up. Always look it up."

First, of course, she had to support them. After she and her husband separated she went to work as a practical nurse. In her free time she made hair switches and transformations. She moved with her daughters briefly to Rockport, on the Maine seacoast, then to Ring's Island, Massachusetts, where Vincent had her tenth birthday, then to Newburyport, where Mrs. Millay herself had grown up. Finally they returned to Maine, settling at last in Camden, which became their permanent home.

In the beginning, Mrs. Millay worked at night so that she could take care of the little girls during the day. When they grew older she worked daytimes as well and also took cases that kept her away from home—often in another town—for days at a time. She soon built up a solid reputation and was greatly in demand.

During the winters, when people became sick more frequently and needed Mrs. Millay's services, the family fortunes rose, while in the summers their income fell off, so that they often were hard put to meet the grocery bills. The girls knew all about their difficulties: Mrs. Millay refused to gloss these over, feeling that only by facing hardships could they learn what life really was.

She saw to it, however, that the girls never lacked what she considered the "important things," and she had strong, unconventional views about these. There were times when they might not have had very substantial meals or quite enough fuel for the cold, grim Maine winters but, whenever possible, the girls had pretty clothes as well as books and the other "impractical" trimmings of a cultivated household. Money was somehow found for piano and singing lessons, music scores, books, paints, magazine subscriptions, and tickets for whatever plays and concerts there were in the area. They had what was probably the best collection of books to be found in any private home in Camden. One of Mrs. Millay's gifts to Vincent, at a time when they could not have had much money, was a set of "twenty-five red books full of knowledge." Vincent was later to say that they always had all of the luxuries of life, "but sometimes few of the necessities."

The neighbors might not always have approved of Mrs. Millay's ideas on how money should be spent or daughters brought up, but she followed her own convictions and encouraged her daughters to do the same. As a family, they had their own viewpoint. When the pipes burst one cold winter, flooding the kitchen floor with water that turned to ice, instead of regarding it as a disaster, the girls put on their ice skates and skated happily on their improvised indoor rink until they all grew warm.

Mrs. Millay was both witty and quick-witted, and the girls developed the same mental agility. Conversation in their household was wide-ranging and rapid-fire—and could take almost any kind of turn. Sometimes it might even end in violent quarreling.

There was an extraordinary combination of interdependence and independence. With their mother gone so much of the time, the girls could come and go as they wanted, with no one to question or check them. They developed a high degree of self-reliance and self-sufficiency. But also, because their mother was absent so much, the girls depended upon each other. They became an extremely close-knit family, warmly and spontaneously affectionate. Vincent's letters to her mother and sisters begin with salutations such as "Dearest Darlings," "My darling sister," "Dearly Beloved" (to Mrs. Millay).

They were fond of nicknames. Edna was called not only Vincent but "Sefe" (short for Josephus), Norma was "Hunk," and Kathleen "Wump" or "Wumpty-Woons." Mrs. Millay was sometimes addressed as "Mumbles." A chafing-dish, given by Mrs. Millay to Vincent, was called "James."

Whenever Mrs. Millay was out on a case, the younger girls were left in Vincent's care. Vincent, a small, thin, quick-moving girl with long red hair, freckled skin, snub nose, and greenish eyes, handled her responsibilities with a brisk and imaginative efficiency. She drew up detailed schedules, dividing the day into fifteen-minute periods, with a particular chore listed for each girl in each period: "Wash dishes," "Study," "Write," "Prepare lunch," "Go into garden." Most meals, however, were spontaneous and unplanned. When it was time to eat, Vincent might send her sisters downtown to buy a feast of pie or other bakery luxuries and milk. If there was no money in the house, she would scrape together some oddly assorted leftovers —perhaps stale cake and pickles or baked beans—and

serve them with tea. Sometimes they would pick blueberries and have them with milk. A friend, invited to
supper by Vincent one day, was startled when "supper"
turned out to be a pan of fudge.

At night she would tell her younger sisters an install-
ment of a continuous story. She kept her mother informed
of their progress: ". . . I am getting along all right in
school but in my spelling-blank I had 10 and 10 and then
9 and I felt auful bad because I thought I would have a
star I am getting along all right and so is Norma and
Kathleens cold is better now . . ." This was written
when she was eight. Later on her reports would include
such items as: "I baked the most delicious bread Fri-
day. . . . Saturday we had baked beans and I had aw-
fully good luck with them. I have made pies, cakes and
doughnuts and we are living almost wholly from home
cooking."

While their mother was away, meals took on the aspect
of the Mad Hatter's teaparty, with the girls using new
batches of clean dishes while the dirty ones piled up until
practically every dish in the house had landed in the sink.
Just before Mrs. Millay's return, the girls, under Vincent's
captaincy, would tear into an orgy of dusting, cleaning,
and dishwashing, the last operation performed to a song
composed by Vincent for the occasion, and ending:

There are pots and pans and kettles galore;
When I think I'm all done there's always some more;
For here's a dozen and there's a score,
I'm the Queen of the Dishpans—hooray!

Visiting friends, attracted by the informality, freedom, and gaiety of this household, would be impressed into service alongside the sisters.

They often made a game of housework. Once the necessity for cleaning up was admitted, someone would call "Corner! Corner!" Each girl would dart to a different corner of the room and clean it, working toward the middle. When they all reached the center, they would turn and finish the fourth corner together.

Actually, Vincent disliked housework. This frenzy of housecleaning was not inspired by a passion for New England scrubbed spotlessness or fear of Mrs. Millay's disapproval. What moved the girls to this magnitude of domesticity was a sense of love and welcome for their mother. Putting the house in order was their way of greeting her. And she responded in kind. When she came home, even if only for a few hours when she was briefly off duty, she never yielded to what must have been an overwhelming temptation to rest. Instead, she went to work with the same bouncy energy as her children, supplementing their domestic accomplishments, mending, washing, and ironing their clothes, and casting an expert eye at the garden.

Whenever Mrs. Millay was home, the girls valued and cherished her presence all the more because it wasn't a matter of daily routine. Perhaps, too, the absence in their daily lives of a father threw more emphasis upon their mother. Although Mrs. Millay never spoke a word against him, her daughters couldn't help being sharply aware that in their family, unlike others, it was their mother who bore all the responsibility, including the heavy economic one, of bringing them up. Whatever the reason, they never took her for granted. And indeed, Cora Millay was not a person to be taken for granted. She was a positive, creative force—altogether the right parent for the kind of poet and person Edna Millay was to become.

3.

Catullus, McGuffey, and Shakespeare

To whom in infancy the sight
Of Sancho Panza and his Knight,
In noble, sad and awkward state
Approaching through the picket-gate,
Was warmer with the flesh of life
Than visits from the vicar's wife;

. . .

For such a child, that distant time
Was close as apple-trees to climb,
And apples crashed among the trees
Half Baldwin, half Hesperides.

—Collected Poems.

ENCOURAGED by her mother and stimulated by the variety and size of Mrs. Millay's library, Vincent entered the world of literature at a very early age. Starting with Mother Goose, she quickly moved on, reading the plays of Shakespeare before she was nine. By twelve, she had read almost all of Tennyson and Milton. During the same period she also read widely in Elizabethan poetry. In addition to her mother's books, Vincent drew heavily upon the collection in the town library.

12

The school curriculum and general cultural atmosphere at the turn of the century gave further encouragement to a child like Vincent. Schoolbooks, like the famous McGuffey's readers, contained selections from many of the best poets and prose writers. The memorizing and recitation of pieces chosen from the great literature of the past was standard practice. There was a good deal of respect for such literature and for the writers who had created it. Vincent acquired this respect along with the habit of reading.

She derived more than just the pleasure of reading verse and a knowledge of poetic technique from the classical English poets. Milton, Shelley, and Wordsworth gave her an early insight into suffering and injustice. She was to say later that during her teens these three poets were "the grist of my mental life," inspiring her to think about problems which she herself had not experienced at that early age, and awakening a social consciousness that was to strengthen as she grew older.

While still a child she began to read Latin verse as well as English, because she enjoyed the sound of it. This love of Latin, which she extended to Latin prose, was to last all her life. When she was fourteen, she spent the summer reading Caesar's *Gallic Wars* by herself and, as an adult, carried a book of Latin poetry—usually Catullus, the only great love poet of ancient Rome—with her wherever she traveled. It went into her suitcase as automatically as her toothbrush; when she was tired, she would turn to Latin verse for relaxation.

When she was twenty, she was asked to draw up a list of authors and books she had read. She wrote: "I've really read so much that I hardly know what to pick out." The list included Shakespeare, Dickens, Wordsworth, Ibsen, Hawthorne, Kipling, Mark Twain, and Tolstoi, among many others.

The range and intensity of her achievement were impressive. When she read a poem she liked, she committed it to memory. What she read became a part of her own intimate experience, so that the life of the imagination and of the mind became almost as tangible as the life she saw in action about her.

Yet she was in no way removed from that life about her. Mrs. Millay, by refusing to overprotect her daughters and by having them share the work and problems of the family, saw to it that they had a strong hold upon reality. Or perhaps it was that reality had a strong hold upon them. Their hardships, while in no sense overwhelming, were concrete enough to intrude upon any vague fantasy world into which they might have wanted to escape. In any case, they had too strong a sense of involvement and enjoyed life too much in all its active forms to want to escape.

Vincent's responsiveness to life in all its manifestations was apparent from the earliest days. She was "obsessed with life," one of her school friends said. She was curious and enthusiastic about everything—every natural phenomenon, every fact, every detail of living, "making a lot of almost nothing." She had an inborn sense of wonder and delight.

She had an equally innate sense of skepticism. She never took anything for granted, but measured it firmly against her own experience and values. She refused to accept pat moral precepts meekly and unquestioningly. When she was a very little girl, someone told her she must never steal apples because stolen apples produced violent stomach-aches when eaten by the thief. She promptly went out, stole some apples, and ate them. There wasn't the slightest intestinal pang as a result and what's more, she said, they were the most delicious she had ever tasted.

When she was older, she told a schoolmate that she cared little what other people thought of her, as long as she could justify her actions to herself. But soon afterward she changed her mind: other people's opinions, she now said, established one's reputation and that *did* matter. When, at another time, she was accused of being inconsistent, she calmly replied, "With consistency a great soul has simply nothing to do."

This independence, this consistent inconsistency which comes of following a pure line of logical thought no matter how far afield it might lead her from either a previous statement of her own or from popular opinion, was to characterize her actions throughout her life. What other people said or did could be accepted only provisionally; ultimately she had to work out the answers for herself. And when she found the answers, nothing could deflect her from acting upon them. Later on, some would criticize this attitude, calling it rigidity or stubbornness; others would praise her, calling it strength of character and integrity. Whatever it was, it gave her solidity and firmness, a kind of New England rockbed to an otherwise volatile personality.

The combination of eager intelligence, curiosity, independence, and a reading experience that outdistanced the regular curriculum was too much for some of her teachers at school. She was a brilliant student, but not always an easy one. Precocious and temperamentally incapable of just sponging up information, she was forever asking questions. Or when questions were asked, her hand always shot up with an insistent eagerness that must have become trying to a teacher who had to cope with a whole class.

One day, in her last year of elementary school, she impetuously darted out of a line. The principal of the school pushed her back into it rather roughly. When Mrs. Millay heard about the incident, she was furious. She came to school herself and, after expressing her unfavorable opinion of the principal, declared that she would not permit her daughter to remain in his school another minute. Taking Vincent with her, she went straight to the office of the superintendent. He listened to the story and then put Vincent directly into the first year of high school.

Coming into a new class in the middle of a term was not easy. Though she could handle the work, there were social difficulties. The other girls had been together before she arrived and, with the clannishness of an already established group, held themselves aloof from the newcomer. They accepted her only gradually, but eventually she established some warm friendships. The first of these was with Stella Derry and soon the two girls were visiting back and forth, eating and sleeping in each other's houses. Stella helped Vincent with math and in return received help from her in Latin and French.

In high school Vincent began to contribute to the school publication, *The Megunticook*. Her first piece was an autobiographical essay called "The Newest Freshman." Poems and other essays followed, and soon she was made a member of the staff, finally becoming editor-in-chief.

In high school, too, she first showed her interest and talent in dramatics, which became another fertile field into which she could turn her imagination loose. She acted in the school plays and wrote a Halloween play which her classmates put on. She received her first theatrical press notice when a local newspaper said of one of her performances: "Vincent Millay was excellent." From time to time touring companies of actors came through Camden. Such theatrical organizations were common in those movieless days. Occasionally they hired local talent for minor roles, and Vincent was often one of the eager applicants. She played parts as varied as that of an old woman or a young boy, and once she was given the juvenile lead.

Her talents were recognized by her classmates. In the class prophecies printed in the high school yearbook, hers read: "There is so much for you to accomplish in the future, so much for your ceaseless ambition to urge you to. Your writing, dramatic ability, and also your singing will serve to assist you in gaining a high position in the world."

There was some jealousy along with the recognition. In the graduating class of 1909, there were thirteen boys and seven girls. When elections for class posts were held, all the boys voted for Henry L. Hall as class poet. No one pretended that Henry was as good as Vincent when it came to writing poetry, but this was a matter of politics, not artistry. The boys resented Vincent. They recognized her superior talents, and did not like her any the better for them. They felt that she had tried "to run things." Now they were getting back at her. The seven girls voted for Vincent, but were defeated. She was not to be class poet.

This was a painful disappointment. She had wanted more than anything to write the class poem and had already begun working on it. Mrs. Millay suggested that she turn in the poem as the graduation paper required from each senior.

Vincent went on to finish her poem, "La Joie de Vivre," and with it won a double victory: when she recited it on graduation night, it received a warm reception from an enthusiastic audience, most of whom thought that it, and not Henry's, was the class poem; and it won a prize of ten dollars.

4.

"Poetical Works
of E. Vincent Millay"

> . . . *the reason I am a poet is entirely because you*
> *wanted me to be and intended I should be, even from the*
> *very first. You brought me up in the tradition of poetry,*
> *and everything I did you encouraged. I can not remem-*
> *ber once in my life when you were not interested in*
> *what I was working on, or even suggested that I should*
> *put it aside for something else.*
> *—From a letter to her mother.*

WRITING poetry, as well as reading it, was an intimate and
natural part of Edna Millay's life almost from the start.
This was her first poem, composed when she was about
five:

> *One bird on a tree,*
> *One bird come to me.*
> *One bird on the ground,*
> *One bird hopping round.*
> *One bird in his nest,*
> *One bird took a rest.*

From the very beginning her mother encouraged her,
listening to what she had written, helping her find the

right word. Vincent was never made to feel that writing poetry was in any way an "odd" or "different" occupation for a young girl. She was never told to "run along and play," or to get on with her homework for school, or to do the dishes, instead of "scribbling." In the Millay household, writing poetry, like playing the piano or singing or painting, was a serious and respected form of expression. Mrs. Millay herself was always trying to find time to write. Whenever she was on night duty and her patient was sleeping quietly, she would spend the long, still hours in writing.

This was not altogether unusual in the Maine of that era. Writing, even the writing of poetry, and certainly the reading and recitation of poetry, were far more natural than they would be in later decades. Girls took elocution lessons, and recited poems as part of an evening's entertainment. Graduating classes intoned verse as part of commencement exercises. People quoted poetry with no self-consciousness or sense of affectation; they wrote it with equal directness. No one hesitated to reveal that he wrote poetry. Indeed, even the small town of Camden was to produce not one but two poets, the second being Vincent's friend and Sunday School teacher, Abbie Huston Evans.

Mrs. Millay recognized Vincent's talent early and made much of it. To the rest of Camden, Vincent was like any other local girl; a bit more sensitive and intelligent, perhaps, but that was all. But to Mrs. Millay, the talent —possibly the genius—was there, and deserved to be encouraged.

Whenever Vincent completed a poem, she copied it carefully and neatly, in ink, into a little brown notebook bearing the label "Poetical Works of E. Vincent Millay." The first page bore a dedication:

To my mother,
whose interest and understanding have been the life of many of These Works, and the Inspiration of many more, I lovingly dedicate this volume.

After that came her first poem, "One Bird," written in a large, round, childish hand. Other poems, including those published in the high school magazine, *The Megunticook*, followed. Her first sonnet was written when she was about fifteen. She entered these early poems until about 1910, and then added an index. The book was put aside until several years later, when she thriftily decided to use the pages still left blank.

Seeing her poems in print must have been another source of encouragement. Some of them appeared in *The Megunticook*, but a far more important medium was the *St. Nicholas Magazine*. This was a unique children's periodical. It contained stories, articles, poetry, and drawings by outstanding writers and artists of the period. Perhaps the most popular section of the magazine was the St. Nicholas League, which printed contributions sent in by the young readers themselves, in order "to encourage boys and girls to give expression to artistic ability through competitive striving." Silver and gold badges were awarded for the best of these contributions. Many who later became famous writers were among the young hopefuls appearing under the heading of the St. Nicholas League.

The Millays were devoted subscribers to *St. Nicholas*, and in due course Vincent sent her poems to the League. The first to be accepted, when she was fourteen, was "Forest Trees." Three more were accepted the following year. One of these, "The Land of Romance," received the Gold Badge. It appeared in March, 1907, and one month later the adult publication *Current Literature*, in its review section on "Recent Poetry," reprinted it with this comment: "The poem that follows seems to us to be phenomenal. . . . Its author (whether boy or girl, we do not know) is but fourteen years of age."

Vincent had signed it, as she did all her poems for *St. Nicholas*, "E. Vincent Millay."

The following year two more of her poems were published in *St. Nicholas*, and the year after that, her "Young Mother Hubbard" received the Silver Badge. The next year, 1910, was the last in which she would be able to contribute, having reached the age limit of eighteen. Her valedictory poem, "Friends," received the top award, a cash prize of five dollars.

With it, she bought a copy of Browning, "whom I admire so much that my prize will give me more pleasure in that form than in any other." She said this in a letter written to *St. Nicholas* to thank the editors for her prize and to say goodbye, concluding with ". . . I am sorry to grow up and leave you." Years later, she recalled this incident when a young member of the League had used *her* cash prize to buy a volume of the poetry of Edna St. Vincent Millay.

Her letter was more than just a polite, routine farewell. Who would publish her now? She would continue to write poetry, but the loss of the *St. Nicholas* as a medium for her work was a serious matter. She knew little of the publishing world and the possible markets for poetry. There seemed nothing for her to do but continue to write entirely for the sake of the writing itself and hope that some day she would be able, as she wrote in a poem when she was fifteen, to "pierce a way into the world's great heart."

5.

The Sense of Hearing

Oh, this is much to ask
Of two delicate ear-drums and of some other perception
Which I do not understand, a little oversensitive
Perhaps to certain sounds.
All my senses
Have broken their dikes and flooded into one, the sense
  of hearing.

—Collected Poems.

EDNA MILLAY once told an interviewer that the conflict in her life had not been the usual feminine one of home vs. career, but of choosing between music and poetry. Her first introduction to the world of art had been through music. Mrs. Millay's concern with singing and opera, and her connection with the town orchestra, had given the girls an easy intimacy with music from their infancy. They had a small Mason and Hamlin parlor organ, which was not only something for Vincent to listen to, but gave her an opportunity, at an early age, to experiment with the creation of sounds herself. Later on the organ was replaced by a real piano.

She was given piano lessons, and proved an exceptional pupil, quick, serious, obviously talented. Even when she

24

was quite small, she was performing skillfully. When she was about twelve a patient of her mother's, John Tufts, heard her play. He had been a noted piano teacher and was now retired, but after hearing Vincent he decided that she was a gifted child who deserved advanced teaching, even if he had to come out of retirement and teach her himself.

Her devotion to music increased, and for the next few years she practiced the piano with as much zeal as she wrote poetry. "I wanted to be a musician and worked passionately at my piano, playing, composing." When she was about thirteen, she put Little Boy Blue into operatic form and set the verses of Mother Goose to music. She and her sisters sang these compositions, sometimes for hours on end, while walking along the country roads in the evening.

Singing was a spontaneous form of expression for the Millay girls. They made up humorous songs, which they sang in parts. Norma had, perhaps, the best voice of the three, a fine, sweet soprano. (She was also the prettiest of the girls.) She was given singing lessons and, later on, sang opera professionally. Vincent's voice was in a lower range. One of their favorite diversions was to sing through entire opera scores, particularly *Aida*. Vincent played the piano, and all three of them sang. When friends came to visit any of the girls, they would sooner or later gravitate to the piano and the song books.

When she was seventeen, Vincent performed at a concert of her own. Mrs. Millay gave her a new dress for the occasion, of yellow chiffon, with a square neck and puffed sleeves ending in metallic bands. She played pieces by Bach, Haydn, Mendelssohn, Godard, and Chaminade. Her interest in music grew more intense than ever.

But all along she had been writing poetry, too, and her skill and absorption in that medium had also been increasing. The *St. Nicholas* prizes added an extra impetus, and in her "small conflict" of the arts, poetry began to pull ahead. One item that may possibly have weighted the result in favor of poetry was the size of her hands. They remained so small that she always had difficulty in reaching over a full octave. There was even some talk of using surgical means to extend her reach.

In the end she was to become a professional poet rather than a concert pianist. But she never ceased practicing. There were periods throughout her life when she "boned away" at the piano for several hours a day. She played ensemble music with friends and neighbors who played stringed instruments. In college she wrote songs and took part in the musical activities of the school. She was to write the libretto for a famous American opera.

Though she never became the concert pianist she once hoped to be, the melody of her lyrics and the presence of extraordinary sound-imagery throughout her poetry would always give evidence of a trained and sensitive ear. A special characteristic of her poetry would be a heightened awareness of sound.

All her life, whenever she was tired or worried, she would go to the piano and play, particularly from Bach or

Beethoven. She committed whole pieces of music to memory—a friend coming to visit her once found her memorizing Beethoven's Fifth Symphony. Music became her refuge. One of her most famous sonnets, "On Hearing a Symphony of Beethoven," begins:

> *Sweet sounds, oh, beautiful music, do not cease!*
> *Reject me not into the world again.*
> *With you alone is excellence and peace,*
> *Mankind made plausible, his purpose plain.*

Years later, when she had become discouraged by the follies and injustice of the world, she was to say that one of the few things which helped her retain her faith in man was his achievement in music. If men had the ability to create beautiful sounds, she felt, then they might also be able to establish a better world.

6.

The Coast of Maine

More sea than land am I; my sulky mind, whipped high
by tempest in the night, is not so soon appeased.
Into my occupations with dull roar
It washes,
It recedes.

—Collected Poems.

THE sea intruded itself very early upon Edna Millay's
consciousness and never left it. Camden was a picturesque little town on Penobscot Bay, with fishing boats
and gleaming white yachts sitting in the harbor. It was
a shipbuilding center. Craft as large as six-masted schoon-
ers were made there, and launching days filled the town
with excitement. Sea captains coming from India and the
Far East brought the outside world into the little port.

It was a wonderful place to grow up in. Camden was
a prosperous town of about three thousand inhabitants,
with quiet, tree-shaded streets, many of them lined with
large, fine old houses. It drew its income not only from
the sea but from the woolen mills and from the summer
visitors who were drawn by the attractions of its loca-
tion and atmosphere. There were iron and brass foun-
dries where the children were allowed to make molds, and
an oakum mill where the children played on coils of old

tarred rope used for making the oakum. There were shells and mussels and driftwood to be gathered on the beaches, and the weed-crusted hulls of old shipwrecks to scramble over. There were sea gulls to watch, and fog bells and the sounds of crashing surf to hear. And there was always the water for swimming and sailing.

But this part of the Maine coast is compounded of more than pretty little villages on a blue-green shore. Unlike the more southern stretches of the Eastern seaboard, here the mountains, rocky, craggy, rugged, come right down to the water, adding strength and vigor to the landscape. High, sheer cliffs rise abruptly from the sea.

There is nothing lush or opulent about the Maine seacoast. It has its pretty spots, its spectacular aspects, but there is more austerity than gentleness on the face of nature in Maine. The calm sea often becomes a wild, gray, angry mass of water beating and breaking around jagged rocks. The summers are short, giving way to grimly cold winters. In Edna Millay's childhood the houses were harder to heat, and the bleak chill of the outdoors often seeped into the interiors just as it did into the crusty natures of the local inhabitants. Even spring in Maine has its own character. When it does return to the ice-locked slopes of the mountains and the frozen coves along the sea, it seems to come almost timidly.

The landscape and the seasons and the climate of Vincent's childhood were as moody and changeable as the sea. A perceptive, intelligent child would be sharply aware of the impact and presence of nature, but it would be a nature very different from the serene meadowslopes of pastoral tradition.

She spent a great deal of her time out of doors, sometimes on solitary excursions up Mt. Battie or Mt. Megunticook, sometimes on walks or picnics with her sisters or a group of friends. The people of Camden used the mountains constantly as part of the terrain of their daily lives. Bird walks in the early, often pre-dawn, mornings were a favorite summer diversion. They would take breakfast along, stopping to eat on a mountain ledge lit by the first rays of the sun, with the ocean spread out beneath them. In the spring Vincent would lead her friends to Mt. Battie, where her own ramblings had disclosed fields of mayflowers. In autumn, when the whole countryside blazed into flame and gold, the girls walked and climbed almost without end.

In summer, the sea became one of the centers of life, and nature as a whole took on a benign and rather social face. This was the time for picnics, swimming, and sailing.

Letters written during these summers to Mrs. Millay (when she was away on a case) are like those of any girl of Vincent's age. They are filled with reports of "fun" activities, generally in the company of other young girls. Details of fishing and boating excursions, of picnics and parties, are described with an almost naïve ebullience. There are several letters which must have been written during the period when she was working on the long, serious poem which first brought her fame, yet these show the same satisfaction over the successful concoction of a shrimp wiggle and the mastery of a seventy-five-foot swim as she might have shown over the completion of a difficult verse passage.

Yet the sea was much more to Edna Millay than a source of summer pleasure. It colored her temperament and permeated the background to her life. The sea appears in her poetry, in direct description as a longed-for aspect of nature, and as a source of symbolic imagery. She could not bear to be away from the sea for long —"I have a need of water near," she was to write. The sight and sound and feel of the sea were basic necessities for her well-being:

> *I have a need to hold and handle*
> *Shells and anchors and ships again!*

But important and pervasive as the sea was, it by no means marked the limit of her response to nature. There were also the mountains rising above Camden, her mother's garden, the nasturtiums that grew along their porch trellis, the herbs they raised and dried, the birds and animals she encountered, even the local vegetables and weeds. They all became as individually known and significant to her as a musical phrase or a line of verse. She learned the names of virtually every bird, flower, herb, tree, constellation, and sea shell that she saw. Her poems are filled with specific names: borage, alkanet, bergamot, hawkweed, blue vervain, yellow charlock, whiteweed, thorn-apple, larkspur, vetch, lupine, strawberry shrub, monkshood, tamarisk, hornbeam, moosewood maple, bobolink, shrike, cuckoo, tree-sparrow, raven, gull, newt, lynx, Vega, Capella, Aldebaran.

This sharp awareness of an immensely varied nature—a nature not always kind or even beautiful—entered into her consciousness and into her poetry. Her very first poem was about birds. When she was twenty, she wrote in a letter to the poet Arthur Davison Ficke, "The earth passion! I have always had that." And several months later, in another letter to him, ". . . you are the only person I know whose poems about flowers and birds and skies and things, filled as they are with your own so evident Earth-Ecstasy, quite satisfy my Earth-Ecstatic soul."

Nature was no vague, generalized, amorphous abstraction to her. It was part of the same intensely felt reality as her mother and sisters, or playing the piano, or sailing a boat, or going to school. A bird was always a real bird to her, not just a convenient symbol of an abstract quality.

She understood that nature was in its place and man in his, and they had a real, concrete, one might almost say practical, relationship to each other. Nature was neither an all-loving, sentimental mother, nor a mysterious, perhaps sinister force. It was impersonal, the source of life and comfort, neither deliberately nor capriciously good or evil. It was an integral, intimate part of her life, from her earliest years. It was to infuse both her life and her poetry with beauty, meaning, and affirmation.

7.

"Renascence"

All I could see from where I stood
Was three long mountains and a wood;
I turned and looked another way,
And saw three islands in a bay.
So with my eyes I traced the line
Of the horizon, thin and fine,
Straight around till I was come
Back to where I'd started from;
And all I saw from where I stood
Was three long mountains and a wood.

—Collected Poems.

WITH the ten dollars that Vincent had won for her graduation poem, she took a trip to Massachusetts in the summer of 1909 to visit her mother's family. Mr. Millay contributed an additional two dollars. In a long letter to Norma and Kathleen, she mentions seeing two musical comedies and describes a visit to an amusement park where she took her first ride on a roller coaster. This letter and others of the same period show that she has already developed an eye for concrete details, an alert ear for sounds, and a sense of quick imagery. "The phosphorus was dazzling: there were spots of it as big as saltines."

When she returned to Camden, there was little for her to do, now that she had graduated from high school. It probably never occurred to her to go on to college— college was not in the pattern for poor young girls living in little Maine towns. She had taken shorthand and typing in high school and spent a summer vacation, when she was fifteen, working as a typist in a lawyer's office. After graduation she worked occasionally as a part-time typist for some of the summer tourists. With her mother still away nursing most of the time she kept house for her sisters, who were now in high school themselves. She practiced the piano and wrote poetry, but by now the possibility of becoming a professional musician had dimmed; and during the year following her graduation, she had passed the age limit of the St. Nicholas League, leaving her with no market for her poems.

In those days she had not yet achieved the sustained periods of beauty that would make such a memorable impression upon those who saw her. To the townspeople, she was "a little redhead" who, like so many adolescent girls, at times looked quite plain, at other times, lovely.

She seems to have had no interest in boys, nor they in her. Her sisters, on the other hand, were very popular. Boys flocked to the Millay household but the attraction was Norma and Kathleen, not Vincent. A large part of her social life centered around the girls' clubs to which she belonged—groups like The Genethod, the S. A. T., and the Huckleberry Finners. This last club consisted of a group of girls who read aloud to each other from

Huckleberry Finn and other books by Mark Twain. After each reading, refreshments were served. The Genethod held their meetings in the parlor of the chapel; they sang, played games, and toasted marshmallows over an open fire. Two of the girls served as hostesses. The S. A. T., standing for Saturday Afternoon Tea, consisted of about six members who took a walk each Saturday afternoon, winding up the excursion with tea served at one of the member's homes.

Vincent took an active part in all these festivities, but this kind of life was quite obviously not enough for a girl of her temperament and talents. Though she was known in town as a bright and lively girl, in whom "the spirit of happiness . . . brightly burned," there were times now when she grew dispirited and restless. She would go off alone to climb Mt. Battie or Megunticook, or to spend hours looking out over the sea. The limitations of life in Camden must have begun to close in upon her. Both she and her mother must have wondered what was to come next and where it was to come from.

Something of how she felt may have been expressed in a long poem she began to write during this period. She was eighteen when she first started "Renascence." Though a poet's work cannot be taken literally as a direct account of his own life, nevertheless it often contains reflections of his experiences and moods, and there are overtones in "Renascence" of Vincent's life at the time of its writing. She had come to a kind of claustrophobic dead-end: there seemed to be nothing on her horizon, nothing in her life but the mountains and sea of Camden. Beautiful though they were, they were boundaries beyond which she could not penetrate.

In the poem she says that no matter where she looked, she came

> *Back to where I'd started from;*
> *And all I saw from where I stood*
> *Was three long mountains and a wood.*

> *Over these things I could not see:*
> *These were the things that bounded me.*

Everything seems to be hemming her in. Not only the mountains, but the sky, all space, all time, the universe itself with all its sorrows and evils seem to press down upon her until she longs for the relief of death.

She imagines herself dead but the sound of the rain pattering on the roof of her grave makes her remember how sparkling and fragrant the earth will be after the rain. She feels an aching longing to be and remain alive— a longing which will never leave her. The rain turns into a storm, and in a violent, thunderous crash of release she finds herself alive and above the earth once more. She hugs the trees and ground, recognizing and accepting with delight the living world. This to her is life's ultimate good, and perhaps its final purpose:

> *God, I can push the grass apart*
> *And lay my finger on Thy heart!*

Her world breaks out of its stifling limitations. It is wide and rich for those who have the breadth of vision or depth of soul to see it. The last lines are filled with the confidence and affirmation that flowed beneath even her most despairing moods:

> *The world stands out on either side*
> *No wider than the heart is wide;*
> *Above the world is stretched the sky,—*
> *No higher than the soul is high.*
> *The heart can push the sea and land*
> *Farther away on either hand;*
> *The soul can split the sky in two,*
> *And let the face of God shine through.*
> *But East and West will pinch the heart*
> *That can not keep them pushed apart;*
> *And he whose soul is flat—the sky*
> *Will cave in on him by and by.*

"Renascence" would have been a tremendous achievement for a poet of any age. For a young girl it was phenomenal. One reader was to call it "part birdsong, part essay in philosophy." It is the overture to all her later work, embodying what were to become her principal themes and techniques. It expresses her feelings about death and her joy at being alive. It is a lyrical rhapsody on nature. At the same time, it reveals her early awareness of suffering and injustice. Her language is simple and concrete, making the dramatic climaxes of the rhymed couplets seem all the more startling.

She worked on the poem for a long time. It was still not quite complete in the early spring of 1912 when her father, who was living in Kingman, Maine, became seriously ill. He had pneumonia, complicated by asthma and a bad heart; and she went to help care for him, taking along the unfinished poem.

While Vincent was in Kingman, Mrs. Millay, who was on a case, noticed one night while watching beside her sleeping patient, a magazine that had been thrown into the wastebasket. Picking it up, she leafed through the pages. A notice caught her eye, and she read it through with mounting interest. It was an announcement of a forthcoming book of poetry, *The Lyric Year,* an anthology which would contain the hundred best poems written in the United States during the year. Three prizes, one of five hundred dollars and two of two hundred and fifty dollars each, were to be offered for the best contributions. Poets were invited to send in their work, not only for the prizes, but also for inclusion in the anthology.

"Now maybe there's a chance for Vincent," thought Mrs. Millay. She wrote her daughter about the competition, urging her to come home at once and submit some of her work. Vincent returned to Camden, finished "Renascence," and sent it, along with several other poems, to *The Lyric Year.*

She was wild with hope. When she told her friend, Abbie Huston Evans, about it, she cried, "Oh, Abbie, wouldn't it be wonderful if I should get in that book!"

Abbie, looking at the excited young girl and aware

of her capacity for being hurt, thought, "You poor child." If Vincent failed in this the letdown would be painful. Yet here she was, one young girl among the thousands of poets entering the contest. The possibility of being accepted for the book, let alone of receiving a prize, seemed infinitely remote.

The first announcement of *The Lyric Year* had appeared in 1911. Since there were so few outlets for the work of American poets, the news stirred great enthusiasm. Manuscripts piled up in the office of the publisher, Mitchell Kennerley. By the time the deadline came around in 1912, ten thousand poems had been received.

Among the judges of the contest was Ferdinand Earle, the editor of the publication. One weekend Earle, assisted by a friend, Professor Donner, was plowing his way through a heap of the manuscripts. Donner, after reading one of them, laughed and tossed it into a wastebasket containing the verse that was to be discarded.

"What's so amusing?" asked Earle. Donner leaned over the wastebasket, picked up the manuscript he had just thrown into it, and read:

> *All I could see from where I stood*
> *Was three long mountains and a wood;*
> *I turned and looked another way,*
> *And saw three islands in a bay.*

Bursting into laughter again, he tossed the pages back into the wastebasket. But Earle's ear had been caught by something. "Hey! That sounds good!" he protested. Donner reached into the basket once more and continued to read aloud from another section of the poem:

> *The world stands out on either side*
> *No wider than the heart is wide;*

"It doesn't sound so bad after all!" he remarked, and went back to the beginning to read it straight through, aloud, not once but twice. To Earle, after all the "insipid and drivelling nonsense" he had been wading through, it seemed like a revelation. He wrote at once to the poet, addressing her as "E. St. Vincent Millay, Esq., Dear Sir," saying he rated her poem so highly that it would undoubtedly receive the first prize of five hundred dollars.

Vincent had been out picking blueberries when the letter arrived. When she returned from the pasture with her pail full, her mother was waiting on the doorstep, holding the letter in her hand. Vincent opened and read it. To the Millays, who could not even imagine what a hundred dollars in one lump would look like, it seemed like the gold at the foot of the rainbow. To Mrs. Millay it was the answer to all her hopes and ambitions; to Vincent it was the beginning of everything she had hardly dared dream about.

She rushed to tell Abbie the news. Jumping up and down, she cried, "Oh, think, Abbie, I'm going to be in that book!"

She was to be in the book, all right, but unfortunately Ferdinand Earle had been premature about the prize. He had practically promised it to Mr. E. Vincent Millay be-

fore the other two judges of the contest had had a chance
to consider the entry. When they did, they disagreed
with him. Yes, it was a fine poem, but no, it was not the
best. It was not even, in their opinion, one of the three
best and hence would not receive even one of the lesser
prizes. It was given fourth place.

Vincent was bitterly disappointed. To have had the
fantastic sum of five hundred dollars so nearly in her
hands and then have it evaporate, was almost too much
to bear. Still, it was very good to have been accepted at
all, and in the meantime, before its actual publication,
"Renascence" achieved another kind of victory for its
composer.

In the summer of 1912 Norma had taken a job as
waitress in the Whitehall Inn, a big resort hotel. Every
summer a ball was given for the waitresses, who were
daughters of the local gentry. Norma invited Vincent to
attend as her guest but Vincent, shy about such matters,
refused. Norma insisted and, in the end, won. Vincent
went to the party. Toward the end of the evening Norma
won another victory. The girls had all been called upon
to display their talents. Some, including Norma, sang;
others performed on the piano. At Norma's coaxing,
Vincent played the piano, including in her repertoire
some songs of her own composition. And finally, a small,
slight, shy figure, speaking in a low and musical voice,
she recited her poem, "Renascence."

In the audience was one of the summer visitors to
Camden, Miss Caroline B. Dow, head of the National

Training School of the Young Women's Christian Association in New York City. She was deeply impressed with the poem and with the poet herself. Until late that night, Miss Dow talked with Vincent. When she learned that Vincent had already graduated from high school and was doing little more than marking time, she urged her to go on to college. She herself, she promised, would do all she could to get the necessary financial assistance.

The world was at last beginning to open out. Perhaps the impact of "Renascence" after its appearance in *The Lyric Year* might have taken her out into the world even if Caroline Dow hadn't "discovered" her. But the particular path opened by Miss Dow provided an immediate entry into a fresh social experience and a new intellectual climate.

8.

The Lyric Year

The fiddles are tuning . . . all over America.
—John Butler Yeats, 1912.

THE year 1912 was decisive in the life of Edna Millay. By a stroke of extraordinary timing, one of several in her life, it was also a year of great significance in the history of American poetry. Nineteen-twelve has been called "the lyric year" and the "dawn of the poetic renaissance." It was a year in which an unprecedented degree of poetic activity took place, a year in which earlier trends in poetry reached their blossoming point and new trends began.

Many of the new trends led away from traditional forms and themes, and gave rise to new schools of poets who sought complete freedom in their creation of new forms. Violent controversies arose, not only between the traditionalists and the experimentalists, but between various groups of experimentalists who fought each other as bitterly as they opposed the traditionalists. The grounds of the quarrels were to shift several times, with the "new" poets finding themselves ranged against even "newer" poets. And some of the most ardent battlers for poetic freedom would harden into authoritarian defenders of their own principles to the exclusion of all others.

43

Through it all there surged a great lyric vitality. The impulses behind this lyric flowering had, of course, been in existence before 1912. The impact of Darwin, Freud, and Marx, the rise of the liberal reform movement, as well as the sheer physical effects of the booming industrialism of the twentieth century, had wrenched a whole generation away from Victorian idealism and gentility. The younger poets were eager to explore what they considered the new reality, and to express their own impressions and interpretations, even when these clashed with traditional beliefs.

By 1912 these impulses had come to a boil in the field of poetry and were straining for outlets. One of these outlets was provided by a new magazine created exclusively for the publication of poetry. This was *Poetry: A Magazine of Verse*, established in 1912 in Chicago by Harriet Monroe, who felt that American poets needed the encouragement that a wider audience would bring. She felt that poets should have a magazine of their own which would pay for contributions, give prizes for outstanding verse, and put no restrictions on forms or themes. Since no such magazine existed, she started one herself, raising the money by getting voluntary contributions from well-to-do Chicagoans. One man, yielding to her plea for money, said: "I don't know any better way to pay my debt to Shelley." Another outlet was offered by *The Lyric Year*, and when the avalanche of ten thousand verses from the impatient pens of two thousand poets poured in upon the editor who was seeking only a hundred poems, the extent of the burst of lyrical energy became apparent.

The impression of a great poetic spontaneous combustion was heightened by the increase in the number of books of verse published. Before 1912 many publishers had turned a cold editorial shoulder to poets; men like Edwin Arlington Robinson and Robert Frost had found it difficult to reach their audience. Now editors and publishers smiled warmly upon poets and printed their work. New firms were established which were friendly to poetry from the start. During 1912 and the years immediately following, books of verse, many of them first books, appeared by Amy Lowell, Robinson Jeffers, Vachel Lindsay, Robert Frost, Edgar Lee Masters, Carl Sandburg, John Gould Fletcher, William Carlos Williams, Conrad Aiken, William Rose Benét, Stephen Vincent Benét, and many others. New anthologies came out. Magazine and newspaper editors began to treat poets with greater respect. They were willing to pay more for poetry and began to feature poems instead of relegating them to the back pages or the ends of columns.

The renaissance of American poetry had started. Beginning in the very same year was the career of Edna Millay, heralded by her poem so auspiciously titled "Renascence." With this poem she suddenly appeared in the American lyrical world, itself just blossoming again. The poet Witter Bynner, writing a few years after the event, described it: "Fully armed, from the head of Jove, had sprung a new miracle. Where there had been nothing, no whisper of her, stood a whole poet. Few were aware, but how aware were those few! Millay became at once a name for them to conjure with . . . a touchstone."

Immediately after the publication of *The Lyric Year*, in November, 1912, there was an eruption of protests over its failure to award a prize to "Renascence." Readers almost unanimously rated it the freshest, the most original, and certainly the best poem in the volume. Edna Millay received as much acclaim as, perhaps more than, if she had won first place. One critic wrote: "The young girl from Camden, Maine, became famous through *not* receiving the prize." Others called her failure to win a prize, "poetry's scandal of the century." Edna received letters from all over the country. One man wrote: "Dear Miss Millay —Your poem is the only one in the book worth a hoot."

Even the prize-winners felt they had won unfairly. Orrick Johns, winner of first place, said his prize was unmerited, "as much an embarrassment to me as a triumph. . . . The outstanding poem in that book was 'Renascence.' . . ." He received sharply worded letters telling him how little he deserved first place. People clipped newspaper and magazine articles criticizing the award and mailed them to him. In the end he refused to attend the award dinner, because "I did not want to be the center of a literary dog-fight." One of the second-prize winners wrote to Edna saying: "I have $250 that belongs to you, any time you ask for it."

Among the other contributors to *The Lyric Year* were

two young men, Witter Bynner and Arthur Davison Ficke, who had already made reputations for themselves as talented poets. They had been classmates at Harvard and were close friends. On Thanksgiving Day, 1912, Bynner was visiting Ficke, then practicing law in Davenport, Iowa. A copy of *The Lyric Year* had just been sent to Ficke. Bynner was glancing through it while walking home from the law office with Ficke. His eye fell upon "Renascence," and, sitting down with Ficke at the base of the Soldier's Monument, he read it aloud.

They had read most of the other poems already, and had grown "somewhat disheartened. . . . And suddenly we stumbled on this one, which really lights up the whole book. It seems to both of us a real vision. . . ." When they reached Ficke's home, Bynner, Ficke, and Mrs. Ficke wrote a joint letter to Edna Millay: "This is Thanksgiving Day and we thank you. . . ."

Though they addressed their letter to a "Miss Edna St. Vincent Millay," they were convinced the name was a pseudonym and that the biographical note at the back of *The Lyric Year* was "a marvel of humor." They wrote to Ferdinand Earle, the editor, saying that the writer of "Renascence" could not possibly be a "sweet young thing of twenty . . . it takes a brawny male of forty-five to do that."

Earle sent this comment on to Edna Millay, who then wrote to Ficke and Bynner: "Gentlemen: I must convince you of your error; my reputation is at stake. I simply will not be a 'brawny male.' " The letter concludes with a P.S.: "The brawny male sends his picture. I *have* to laugh."

This set off a lifelong correspondence and friendship with Ficke and Bynner, especially with Ficke, who sent her books, gave her advice, discussed her poetry, and became, as she put it, her "Spiritual Advisor." In one of his first letters, written in December, 1912, he asked if she had gotten some line from a book. She replied indignantly: "I'll slap your face. I never get anything from a book. I see things with my own eyes, just as if they were the first eyes that ever saw, and then I set about to tell, as best I can, just what I see."

By the beginning of 1913 it was settled that she was to go to college. The school chosen was Vassar, with some preliminary work at Columbia University's Barnard College in New York City.

She reached New York at the beginning of February, 1913, and found it a city of buildings, ". . . buildings everywhere, seven & eight stories to million and billion stories . . . and *noise*, yes, in New York you can *see* the noise." She was almost twenty-one, and this was her first visit to a large city. After the quiet, low-roofed towns of the Maine seacoast, with their wide horizons opening out over the sea, New York must have seemed formidable, and she never lost a faint sense of unease in its busy streets.

She lived at the Residence of The National Training School of the Y.W.C.A., the school of which Caroline

Dow was the head. Immediately after her arrival she enrolled at Barnard College, where courses started almost
at once.

Her plunge into the life of New York City started almost at once, too. Everyone wanted to meet the young
girl whose poem had stirred such a controversy. Even before she left Camden, established poets and critics had
sent her invitations to visit them when she reached New
York. The Poetry Society of America gave a lunch for
her, at which she finally met Witter Bynner in person.
Edna was still so shy that she could not bring herself to
read "Renascence" aloud, and Bynner read it instead
while she sat quietly on the sofa, listening.

The poet Sara Teasdale, eight years older than Edna
and already a minor celebrity, sent a note inviting her to
tea. Edna, who had read and admired Sara Teasdale's
work, accepted eagerly. They met for tea and liked each
other immediately, so the tea was shortly followed by
dinner and then by a ride on the upper deck of one of
the big two-decker buses that ran along Riverside Drive.
Almost twenty years later Sara Teasdale would write: "I
like to think that when I first read you, long ago, I knew
you and named a star."

In between the parties at which Edna was presented
to the current literary lions, and her classes at Barnard,
she managed to see a good deal of New York. She went
to see the controversial exhibition of modern art, the
famous Armory Art Show, first of its kind in America,
where she decided that the work of the Cubists "looks

like piles of shingles." She went to see Sarah Bernhardt in *Camille*—"I'm all gone to pieces. . . ." she wrote home after seeing Bernhardt. It was all immensely stimulating and fantastically different from Camden, Maine.

She also began to meet young men, so many of whom were to be drawn to her by the irresistible combination of wit, intelligence, and femininity which was now becoming evident. One of the first of these young men was Salomón de la Selva, a young Nicaraguan poet, who was lecturing on modern poetry at Columbia University while she was attending Barnard. He became her companion on many of the exploratory trips through New York, on the Fifth Avenue bus rides, and on ferry trips to Staten Island. Taking rides on ferries and on the upper deck of the old Fifth Avenue buses were among the favorite diversions of the impecunious young people of the city; and of all the ferries ringing Manhattan at the time, the Staten Island ferry was the most preferred. It gave the longest ride for the price (five cents), and one could always get off on the Staten Island end to stroll through the wildest country available so near New York, or swim and picnic on an isolated beach. One of these ferry trips, presumably taken with Salomón, became the subject of the poem "Recuerdo" (Remembrance), which Vincent was to write later.

All this time she kept on writing. She finished and sent two poems to the *Forum*, and started a short story which was later sold to *Smart Set*. Early in April she received a letter from the *Forum*, and when she opened the envelope there was a "pinky-lavender slip," the first check she had ever received, breaking her "hoodoo of 'all praise and no profit.' "

The check was for twenty-five dollars. She kept it for a few days just to look at, and then mailed it off to her mother. "Promise me, please," she wrote, "that with some of this you'll do something to make something easier for yourself. Shoes, dear,—or have your glasses fixed if they're not just right. . . . And I'd like it so much if each one of you would get some little tiny silly thing that she could always keep."

Her triumphs continued. People sent her books and letters. Poets corresponded with her. Arthur Ficke, an authority on Japanese art in addition to being a poet and lawyer, sent her his book of poems, *Twelve Japanese Painters*. A young man living in Texas sent her some of his verses, entitled "To a Spring Flower." A Princeton man wrote a letter congratulating her on her "articulation of a mood essentially inarticulate."

If she had wanted, she probably could have remained in New York and taken her place immediately in the literary life of that city, and proceeded to advance her career and reputation without further delay. But she had set her course for Vassar and allowed nothing to deflect her.

At the end of the school term at Barnard, she returned to Camden to spend the summer preparing for the Vassar entrance examinations in the fall of 1913. She had to work hard on mathematics and history. She also studied

Latin, with tutoring assistance by mail from a Vassar professor, Elizabeth Hazelton Haight, who was to become her close friend as well as teacher once she was at the college itself.

But though she was back in Camden again, there was no feeling of being hemmed in. The world was opening up for her. New York, she wrote to Arthur Ficke, now seemed "just across the yard, you know, in everything but distance."

9.

Vassar

We see in the Times
That pickled limes
Are Vassar's delight,
And at the fall of the night
To see the Seniors weeding the begonias in the circle
Is a beautiful sight,
It is a beautiful sight;
Oh! the daisy-chain marshal wears a rose and gray dress
That cost a million dollars, not a red cent less,
(The Post *inserts this item as they gallop to press.*)
—*From "The Patient Periodical."*

SHE took the examinations and was able to enter Vassar in the fall of 1913. Caroline Dow had taken care of the financial arrangements, which included a Scholarship Aid from the college, just as she had raised the money for the preliminary period at Barnard.

Vincent Millay, as she was known at Vassar (the name Edna hardly appears in the college annals), was then twenty-one years old, about four years older than the average entering freshman. In experience, background, and probably in sheer intellectual capacity as well, the gap was even greater. She had been brought up to be unusually independent and self-reliant; she had already received public acclaim for her talents and had been the center of a literary storm; she had already shown herself capable of sustained creative activity. To Vincent the "don'ts" and "mustn'ts," the rigidly pre-scribed courses of study, the great hedge of rules and restrictions which existed then, all provided by the authorities of a girls' college for the protection of their tender young charges, must have seemed ridiculous and irksome.

There was an elaborate system of cuts and absences, involving a great amount of record keeping. Young men were permitted on the campus only on Sundays, and then only under heavy chaperonage. When an intrepid male did make his way into this fortress of women, windows would open and heads would pop out so that the girls could get a clearer view of this rare phenome-non.

For almost the first time in her life, Vincent came up against rules and bans that had never been applied even by her mother during childhood. At home in Maine she had been free to yield to virtually any impulse; here she found that what appeared to her as a perfectly simple and logical action, like getting up in the middle of the night to walk on the moon-drenched campus, aroused horrified protests. Smoking was completely banned—a restriction she evaded by taking her cigarettes off-campus to a nearby cemetery.

She cut classes with almost as much regularity as most

students attended them. She refused to take attendance requirements seriously and took pleasure in inventing deliberately far-fetched excuses for her continual absence from classes or chapel. When chapel was missed, a written excuse had to be presented on a specially provided form. With most of the girls the excuse was generally illness, but Vincent would write: "It was raining and I was afraid the red on the pew cushions would fade on my new dress." Or: "I was so engrossed in my math, which Miss S. makes so fascinating, that I didn't hear the chapel bell," despite the openly known fact that she hated math and scarcely did any work in it at all.

When she didn't miss a class altogether, she often arrived outrageously late. There was one freshman history class which she would regularly enter after the session was two-thirds over. The teacher would pause, lose her place, become flustered, and then finally resume the interrupted lecture while Vincent settled herself in her seat with a calculated air midway between embarrassment and insouciance. This went on day after day, and the class, according to one of its members, "wickedly enjoyed the daily drama."

This kind of conduct infuriated many of her teachers. They were as unable to understand or condone her cavalier disdain of the strict attendance required as she was unable to accept their insistence on an inflexible regimen. They were even more confused when at the end of the term, having put herself through intensely concentrated cram sessions, fortified by vast amounts of black coffee through several consecutive nights, she would turn in first-rate examinations and term reports.

She had a phenomenal memory. If necessary, she could memorize virtually the entire contents of a book. Just before her geometry examination at the end of her first year at Vassar, she brought the course textbook to Harriett Weiffenbach, with whom she shared the third floor of an off-campus Freshman House. "Quiz me on it," she demanded. Harriett asked her a question. "That is the top of page 64," Vincent replied, and then repeated the entire theorem and its solution word for word.

One year she had a Spanish class which met at 8:30. This was far too early for her; most mornings, instead of getting up for class, she would turn over and go back to sleep. At the end of the first term her classmates wondered how she could possibly pass the exam. But before the final, she stayed up all night studying not just the section of the textbook for the first semester, on which the examination was to be, but the entire book, covering the second term as well. The next day she turned in the best paper in the class.

Henry Noble MacCracken, Vassar's new young President, had his own troubles with her. She was enrolled in his course in the drama. One day she sent him a note explaining that she was too ill to attend his class that morning. Later that same day he came across her at one of the college gates, trying to prove to the gatemen that she could kick high enough to hit the light. Dr. Mac-Cracken commented on her "quick recovery from illness." She replied: "At the time of your class, I was in pain with a poem!"

The composition of poems, some of which she sold while still at college, was given as her principal justification for cutting classes. Indeed, her absorption when in the act of writing was so intense that the details and requirements of the normal world around her faded away completely. One Saturday morning she arranged with Harriett Weiffenbach to go out on some errands. After breakfast Harriett went to Vincent's room and found her sitting at her study table, a piece of gold silk brocade around her shoulders, writing a sonnet with a long quill pen. Her room was in a mess, but Vincent had forgotten it as completely as she had forgotten Harriett, Vassar, and the rest of the world.

"A poem is like a child, you know," she once told the Head Warden, "when it is time for it to be born it has to have attention."

But many of her teachers remained unconvinced or at least unimpressed, and carried their complaints to the President. He would send for Vincent and there would be a tearful scene in his office. In those days tears were quite common among young ladies, and even among the not-so-young ladies on the faculty, and Dr. MacCracken always kept extra handkerchiefs in his desk drawer. ("Vassar tears flowed like a river. I sat silent and miserable while student or teacher wept on," wrote Dr. MacCracken.) On at least one occasion, two beautifully laundered handkerchiefs were returned to Mrs. Mac-

Cracken by Vincent, with the message ". . . tell him that I washed and ironed them myself."

Finally, Dr. MacCracken called her into his office and informed her that no matter what she did, he would not expel her. "I know all about poets at college," he said, "and I don't want a banished Shelley on my doorstep!"

She stared angrily out the window for a few minutes, and then replied, "On those terms, I think I can continue to live in this hell hole."

At the beginning of 1914 she wrote to Arthur Ficke, "I hate this pink-and-gray college! . . . They treat us like an orphan asylum. They impose on us in a hundred ways and then bring on ice-cream.—And I hate ice-cream."

But by the end of her first year, in May, 1914, she was writing home: ". . . I'm crazy about the college. . . ." Once she had adjusted herself more or less to the requirements of an organized, rule-ridden institution, she was able to enjoy and take advantage of qualities at Vassar which must certainly have been lacking in Camden. For all the limitations imposed by the mere fact of being a girls' school with Victorian hangovers, Vassar was, nevertheless, a stimulating campus. When Henry Noble MacCracken arrived there, he found the quality of teaching "definitely better than that I had known at either Harvard or Yale."

Vassar was involved in the movement for the emancipation of women, one of the burning issues of the day.

By 1915 the suffragist movement had been revivified and was reaching a new height of aggressive activity. President MacCracken had become an ardent supporter of votes for women after hearing the famous English suffragists, Emmeline Pankhurst and her daughter Christabel, speak to a hostile crowd in Hyde Park, London. He decided that "a few men on their side might help," and forthwith became one of those few men. One of the American leaders of the movement was Inez Milholland, called the "Amazon beauty," who had graduated from Vassar in 1909. In 1915 she returned to visit her old campus and was welcomed with enormous enthusiasm by the undergraduates, among whom was Edna Millay. Even girls who had been apathetic to the suffragist movement were stirred to its support by the impression made upon them by Inez Milholland. She was, incidentally, accompanied by her husband, Eugen Boissevain, who was to appear again, more dramatically, in Vincent's life.

In later years, when Dr. MacCracken was asked about Vincent Millay, he said that she had been "by fits an extraordinarily good student, then extraordinarily bad." As she had done in high school, she frequently interrupted the work of the class or the lectures of her teachers to ask acute questions or to point out what seemed to her to be their errors. When they showed resentment at these tactics, she was baffled, feeling that mature scholars should be dedicated to the selfless and impersonal pursuit of truth.

Nevertheless, despite their difficulties with her uncompromising spirit, many of her teachers found her a brilliant and even, at times, a highly satisfying student. In the courses which interested her, she paid close and intelligent attention. Her own contributions to class discussions would often, in the words of one of her teachers, "electrify a class." Her papers were excellent; even her exams were apart from the ordinary run of such documents. A history examination now preserved in the Vassar library shows a clear, organized intelligence, with the formal answers enlivened by informal comments upon her own replies. In response to one question she gives the required answer about how to remedy a certain situation, and then adds in parenthesis: "Of course you can't." In another reply she includes a passionate personal diatribe against prejudice. Throughout the exam she writes in an incisive prose style that would refresh the heart of any teacher accustomed to the general literary level of college examination booklets. However, in classes which failed to ignite her interest and which she took only to fulfill requirements, she was openly bored, to the irritation of both the instructors and the other students.

Most of her courses were in English literature, with foreign languages and literatures running a close second. She studied Greek and Latin, French, German, Italian, and Spanish.

She had a special feeling for languages. About three weeks after entering Vassar, she told her German instructor that though this was her first chance at German, "by Christmas I shall be the best in the class." The instructor later wrote that she became easily the best, not by Christmas, but by Thanksgiving. Vincent's assurance of success was prompted not by conceit but by an honest assessment of her own abilities. She was never guilty of a false or misapplied modesty.

Vassar was a singing and acting college, imbued with what President MacCracken called "creative gaiety." The girls sang at mealtimes and at parties, they did "step singing" in front of the college buildings, and sang marching songs and serenades at night. They sang every form of classical and popular composition and made up their own songs. Each class assembled a song book, sometimes containing over a hundred original pieces. There were special songs composed for special occasions. The grand climax of all this lyrical outpouring came at the annual Class Song Contest on Founder's Day, one of the biggest events on campus.

When the girls were not singing, they were acting. In addition to the ambitious works put on by the classes in Dramatic Production, there were also plays performed by the English, music, and language departments, by each class, by the literary society, and by the individual residence Houses. The faculty got into the act, putting on its own play on Founder's Day, and members of the faculty often took roles in student productions.

There must have been at least one play a week, while the singing never stopped. It was a wonder, observed President MacCracken, that any academic work got done at all. For Vincent this preoccupation with singing and dramatics provided ready-made outlets for the talents and interests which had filled her earlier years. She took part in everything: writing and singing songs, writing and acting in plays. Her ability was quickly perceived and welcomed, and she was often called upon to devise songs and skits for all kinds of occasions.

During her second and third years at Vassar she lived in a corner room on the fifth floor of what was then North Hall. Many of the girls here became her close friends, particularly Charlotte Babcock, Anne Gardner, and Frances Stout. Vincent often entertained the girls by playing the piano and singing for them. One day, while a group of girls were gathered in the living room, the wind began to blow fiercely, black storm clouds covered the sky, and a heavy rain pelted down. As suddenly as it had begun, the storm ended, the sky cleared, and the sun came out. Vincent sat down at the piano and improvised a song of joy about the ending of the storm and the reappearance of the sun.

In her second year she wrote the words for the Sophomore Tree Ceremonies of 1915, considered "the best they ever had here." The next year her original song, "The Patient Periodical," won the Class Song Contest on Founder's Day. Her last college composition was the famous Baccalaureate Hymn, "St. Vincent," for which she wrote both the words and music.

Vincent's first appearance on the Vassar dramatic scene was when she recited, in Latin and nestling in her hands a dead song-sparrow borrowed from the Museum of Natural History, Catullus's "Passer Mortuus Est" at a classical soirée given by a group of students. Soon she was taking a leading part in the regular dramatic activities of the college.

She became one of the best actresses in the school. Her voice was low and resonant, with an unusual and unforgettable quality, and she could throw herself completely into any kind of role. She appeared in one play after another, gaining the admiration not only of the college audience but of the dramatic critics of the local Poughkeepsie newspapers. By her senior year she had an adoring following of younger students who often brought her flowers when she appeared in a play.

During her last year she took a course in playwriting and spent a good deal of time working on her own plays. She would copy them out on her typewriter, stopping occasionally to read a few lines to whoever was around to listen. She would ask "Isn't that clever?" and then proceed to explain just why it was so good.

The first of these was a one-act play called *The Princess Marries the Page*. It was performed by the class, with Vincent taking the leading role. *The Wall of Dominoes*, the only play she ever wrote in prose, took first prize in the competition held by the Association of Northern College Magazines. Then came *Two Slatterns and a King*, inspired by the medieval morality plays. After she graduated she was asked by the Vassar College Alumnae Association to write a play for their fiftieth anniversary celebration and responded with *The Lamp and the Bell.*

Her experience with college dramatics led her to think seriously of a career in the theater. As her graduation approached, she felt the shortage of money keenly and began to consider the problems which would face her after college. She wrote to her family: "I wish I had some money. . . . I *must* sell some poems . . ."

All through college she had continued to write and sell her poems. She sold them to leading magazines and they appeared in several important anthologies of verse. She planned to publish a book of her poems soon after graduation. She was also active in academic poetry circles: one of her poems, "Suicide," received a prize in an intercollegiate poetry contest. Together with "Interim" it appeared in the *Vassar Miscellany.* There was a little difficulty at first with "Suicide" when some of the faculty were shocked, considering the subject unsuitable for a college girl. Arrangements were made for her to recite the poem to a group of faculty members; they were pacified by the moralistic ending in which God chides the suicide: "Thou hadst thy task, and laidst it by. . . ."

She took it for granted that once she had left college and was out on her own, she would gravitate to New York instead of returning to Camden. The plans which were beginning to buzz around in her head included transplanting her entire family to New York. She felt that Norma must have her "chance" too. Norma was very skillful at sewing and Vincent felt that she should come to New York and study design. Kathleen was already being given her chance. She had been sent to the Hartridge School in New Jersey to prepare her for entering Vassar, which she did in 1917.

By the time Vincent reached her senior year, she had become a distinctive figure on the campus. She was an outstanding college actress and playwright and one of the best songwriters (probably one of the best singers, too) in the school. As a result of her cleverness the class of '17 scored several great successes in the competitive song activities.

Though she was almost steadily engaged in writing and publishing poetry, she talked very little about this aspect of her life to her college friends. Few of them were aware of her literary connections outside the college. To most of the girls she was another student, more brilliant and talented than most, with a magnetic personality, but still a student.

Her own immediate friends found her a wonderful companion: her witty, nimble mind and spontaneous high spirits made Vincent, they said later, a joy to be with. She could be delightfully silly and "added greatly to the color and fun of our daily lives." Anything could stimulate her—the dogwood in bloom, the flames of a bonfire. One of her college friends said afterward that she seemed to hear, feel, taste with more intensity than the average girl so that any experience or excursion shared with her—even running across the lawn to the library—took on a new dimension.

Her friends loved to hear her talk about her family and childhood, which had been so different from theirs. She would make them laugh with her demonstrations of the Maine dialect. But she had an equally avid curiosity about their lives. One day someone mentioned the childhood games of jacks and mumblety-peg, which she had never played. Here was a gap in her experience which had to be filled! Someone got hold of a ball, jacks, and pocketknife, and for an entire spring, whenever they had any free time, she and her friends would sit down behind a pillar on the smooth tile floor of the Chapel entrance and play jacks by the hour. Or they would move onto the nearby grass lawn and play through several series of mumblety-peg throws with their jack-knife. She was fascinated by these little games and could not seem to get enough of them.

In return, she tried to introduce the girls to some of the winter pleasures of her Maine childhood. She loved cold, wintry weather and at the first sharp drop of the thermometer or after the first heavy snowstorm, out would come her ice skates or snowshoes, and off she would go. Like the sea, snow and frost were elements she had grown up with, and she reveled in them.

Her sense of the dramatic—and her need to dramatize —were always in evidence. Whenever she had stockings to darn she would go into Harriett Weiffenbach's room and say, "Let me have your ring." Harriett would give her a gold ring in which the stones were set flush in a heavy gold mounting, and Vincent would put it on her finger with the stones turned toward her palm, so that it looked like a wedding ring. "Now," she would say, "I feel like the mother of six children so I can do my darning." This was the only way that she could bring herself to do it.

Not all the students responded to her with equal enthusiasm. There was, perhaps, a tendency to regard with suspicion someone so original, unconventional, and ahead of the times. Some of the girls resented what they considered her histrionic exaggerations in class, her occasional lapses of consideration for her teachers or classmates when she openly showed her boredom. She could behave with great indifference toward some people. If there were no immediate meeting of the minds, or of wit, imagination, or sympathy between herself and someone else, she would lose all interest and withdraw from any possible relationship.

But when her interest or affection was aroused, there was no limit to her warmth and responsiveness, no matter who aroused it. She was sometimes seen chatting with the maids from whom, she told her friends, she felt she learned a great deal. Once she wrote a note to the maid about cleaning her room, ending it with:

> *Won't you come in bye and bye*
> *And sweep the cobwebs from my sky?*

Though young men on the campus itself were a notable rarity, nevertheless she did manage to see something of them. There was Salomón de la Selva, now teaching Spanish at Williams College in Massachusetts. He spoke so glowingly of her to his colleagues that one of them, Professor Rice, and his wife invited Vincent to spend a weekend at Williamstown. There were other young men, including "Scrubby" Moore, a friend of Charlotte Babcock's fiancé, with whom Vincent would make a foursome. She continued to correspond with Arthur Ficke during her years at Vassar, though she had still not met him in person.

Vincent Millay wound up her college career in a last great furor of violated rules, outraged faculty reactions, and blazing class emotions.

The prologue to the final event took place during the spring recess of 1917, in Vincent's last semester before graduation. She spent the vacation in New York City. A friend invited her to the opera to hear Caruso in *Aida*. Vincent knew the opera by heart and could play every note of the score. To hear it sung professionally would be a great event for her; and with Caruso appearing in it, the opportunity became irresistible. Unfortunately, the date of the performance fell two days after she was due back at school. The combination of Caruso and *Aida* was too much for her, however—she remained in New York and had a glorious time.

When she returned to Vassar, she was penalized for her late return by being "campused," which meant, chiefly, that for the rest of the term she would not be permitted to leave the campus overnight. Almost two months passed with no further incident. But one beautiful Saturday toward the end of May, two of Charlotte Babcock's friends drove up in a little Saxon car and invited Charlotte and Vincent to go for a ride. Back in 1917 a car was still an exciting novelty and, once again, Vincent could not resist temptation.

They drove across the river and through the spring countryside, with Vincent composing verses about the radiantly blooming cherry and peach trees and all the girls singing and laughing—"We just yelled for joy," said Charlotte later. One of Charlotte's friends, the daughter of a minister, invited the group to her home to have dinner and spend the night. After dinner they went to a movie and then returned to sit by the fire.

The next morning the girls drove around the newly built Ashokan Reservoir and stopped at an inn for coffee. In her account of the incident, Charlotte said, "I don't remember whether or not we all signed our names in the guest book, but Edna St. Vincent Millay did . . ."

It was that signature which caused all the trouble. It converted a harmless episode into a Vassar *cause célèbre*, and laid the groundwork for a score of wildly exaggerated tales which still color the memory of Vincent Millay's graduation from Vassar.

Several days after the girls had been there, a Vassar warden stopped for lunch at the inn and saw the signature. She remembered that Vincent was still "campused," and reported her discovery to the college authorities. The faculty voted to suspend Vincent indefinitely. This was just before Commencement, which meant that she would not be permitted to attend the ceremonies, even though a large part would consist of her own contributions. She had written the words and music for the Baccalaureate Hymn, the words of the Tree Ceremonies and of the Marching Song—yet they would all go on without her.

She was devastated. "My diploma will be shipped to me . . ." she wrote home, "like a codfish—& it all seems pretty shabby, of course, after all that I have done for the college, that it should turn me out at the end with scarcely enough time to pack and, as you might say, sort of 'without a character.' " She left the campus and went to stay at the nearby home of Dr. Elizabeth Thelberg, the college physician, while students and faculty hotly debated the situation.

Vincent's classmates drew up petitions and collected letters of protest for presentation to Dr. MacCracken. "It was," wrote Vincent, ". . . a splendid row."

In the midst of all the excitement, rehearsals were begun of the Baccalaureate Hymn, and it turned out that no one knew it well enough to conduct the rehearsals. She was permitted to return to the campus for one hour a day to direct the class in her song, though she was barred from its performance on Baccalaureate Sunday.

Dr. MacCracken was in a quandary. Although he had the power of veto in faculty action, he had resolved never to use it. However, he finally decided to apply it in this one case, the only time in his career as President.

He lifted the suspension and allowed her to return for the remainder of the exercises.

"I was ashamed not to have acted earlier," he said, "for there were few students who had done more for their college than this young poet."

Standing in her cap and gown, she received her diploma from the hands of a warmly smiling President. "Commencement went off beautifully," she wrote home, "& I had a wonderful time." She signed the letter, "Vincent (Edna St. Vincent Millay A.B.!)."

10.

Interim

Seems as if somewhere there ought to be something for me, doesn't it?
—From a letter written home, September 22, 1917.

HER first plans after graduating from Vassar in June, 1917, centered around getting a job as an actress. She would continue writing poetry no matter what else she did, but for immediate bread and butter purposes she turned to the theater. During the spring recess which she had spent in New York (when she had overstayed for two days in order to hear *Aida*), she had an interview with the manager of the Washington Square Players, one of the new "little theater" groups in Greenwich Village.

Nothing came of the interview. In June, with the disputed Commencement happily concluded and her diploma safely received, she went back to New York City to look for work again. But again she was unsuccessful and decided to go home. She wrote to Norma that it was a bad time to look for a job, her wardrobe needed refurbishing, it was hot, the city was expensive, she had some writing to do. She would spend the summer in Camden and then return to New York in the fall.

As it turned out, she did not spend the entire summer at home. While at Vassar, she had met the actress Edith Wynne Matthison, who used to visit the college and give professional assistance to its dramatic workshop. They had established a close friendship. Edith Matthison and her husband, the playwright Charles Rann Kennedy, invited Edna to spend part of the summer with them. At the end of August, Edna went to stay with the Kennedys in New Hartford, Connecticut. She had "the most wonderful time,—oh, *wonderful!*"

While she was there, she put the finishing touches to her first book of poems, which she had been preparing for publication. It was to be issued by Mitchell Kennerley, the publisher of *The Lyric Year.*

Around the middle of September she went on to New York, staying in the Kennedys' apartment there for several weeks. Once again she made the round of theatrical producers, and again with no results. One manager said he would like to give her a secondary part, but unfortunately her hair was too near the color of the leading actress's. "Seems as if *somewhere* there ought to be something for me, doesn't it?" she wrote home plaintively.

In the meantime she kept going financially by giving readings of her poems. She did not need very much— staying at the Kennedys removed the rent problem, and frequent invitations to dine out cut down her food bills. Both Professor Haight and Edith Matthison helped her get the reading engagements by speaking about her to their friends. One of these was Mrs. Blanche Hooker, a friend of Professor Haight's, in Greenwich, Connecticut. Edna's trunk hadn't arrived, and so Mrs. Hooker "dressed me up in something of hers, a gown with a train & hanging about six inches on the floor all around, made out of three rainbow colored scarfs." This was to have a lasting influence on her reading performances, for from then on she always made her professional appearances in long, trailing gowns. She wanted something "long & drapy . . . very graceful & floaty." She loved beautiful clothes and rich colors and wore them so well and with such distinction that even during the years when she had practically nothing to spend on them, she always created an impression that far exceeded the actual quality of the clothes themselves. Most of all, she loved beautiful shoes. They were her one extravagance. Even if her clothes were old or made over, she did not mind as long as her shoes were good.

She received no money for her first reading, which was a sort of preliminary trial engagement. But Mrs. Hooker was so satisfied with the results that she immediately asked her to give another performance, "for which," wrote Edna to Charlotte Babcock, "I was paid the fabulous sum of fifty dollars—Charlie, it wasn't worth fifty cents; you know, I just sat in a chair & said them as I used to do for you kids sometimes,—but it was a wealthy woman's beautiful gracious way of helping me along.—Oh, my *God*, people are so good & kind to me!"

Right after that, she went to the Bennett School, near Vassar, at the recommendation of the Kennedys who were connected with the school. She spent a week there helping with the production of her plays, *The Princess Marries the Page* and *Two Slatterns and a King*, and giving a reading of her poetry one night. She received another fifty dollars for her week's work.

Between reading and job-hunting she attended plays and concerts, went to meetings of the Poetry Society, dined out with friends, and went out with a series of young men, including Salomón de la Selva ("we raise the devil") and Harrison Dowd (who asked her, "How does it feel to be a success?").

She was offered jobs, but nothing that she really wanted. One family asked her to serve as a governess for their children, an offer she turned down. Mrs. Thompson, "a lovely woman who helped put me through college," who had a good deal of faith in Edna's future as a poet, then asked her to be her secretary. Caroline Dow wanted Edna to take the job, but, much as she disliked going against the wishes of Miss Dow and Mrs. Thompson, she was reluctant to give up her independence, feeling that she would be unable to write if she were always conscious of the demands, however light, the job would make upon her.

But toward the end of October she changed her mind and went up to Sparkhill, to the Thompsons. Here, far from spending all her time addressing envelopes and answering the phone as she had feared, she discovered that nothing was expected of her at all, unless she wanted to help arrange the flowers. Mrs. Thompson's sole purpose in asking her to come as "secretary" was to give her a chance to rest and write. She was even served breakfast in bed every morning.

This comfortable interlude lasted for several weeks and then she was back in New York again, making plans to dig in seriously. Norma was to join her—Edna sent twenty-five dollars for her expenses—and the two sisters would face the city and the future together. It would be hard, she wrote to Norma, but she felt they would succeed and was, she said, "all enthusiasm & good courage." By December, Norma had joined her in New York.

In December, too, her first volume of poetry, *Renascence and Other Poems*, came out. It was a thin book, attractively bound in black with gold letters. The Vassar students backed the book strongly, promising Edna to give it to each other as Christmas presents.

The book, added to *The Lyric Year* affair, helped establish her reputation, although it was still hard for her to believe in that reputation. In a letter to Charlotte Babcock at this time, she wrote: "My poem is out in the Century today—feel so grand!—if you see it hunt up the front where it says I am one of 'the best known younger American poets'—! I didn't know anybody had even heard of me. . . ." But people in growing numbers were hearing about her, and it was not entirely as an unknown that she was entering the next stage of her life.

11.

The Village

There was a Greenwich Village then—
A refuge for tormented men
Whose heads were full of dreams, whose hands
Were weak to do the world's commands;
Builders of palaces on sands—
These, needful of a place to sleep,
Came here because the rents were cheap.
                                    —Floyd Dell.

WHEN Edna Millay had come to New York for the first time in 1913, the poetic renaissance was in full swing. By 1917 it had reached its height, and a new mood was about to sweep the country. One of its great centers was that part of New York City known as Greenwich Village, and one of its embodying spirits was to be Edna St. Vincent Millay.

Back in Revolutionary days the little village of Green Wich was a pleasant country spot two miles up the river from New York. As New York expanded northward, the village became a part of the city itself. But even after it had been absorbed by the developing metropolis, it retained a distinct flavor of its own. Its crooked little streets, curved or oddly angled, did not fit in conveniently with the northward-pushing avenues set out in straight uncompromising lines, and the city builders found it expedient to bypass the Village altogether. So it quietly remained off to one side while the city grew. As time went on and newer and higher structures and more and noisier traffic filled the city proper, the small old red-brick houses and narrow crooked streets of the Village became a peaceful and picturesque, if slightly run-down, backwater. It became a haven for those looking for an inexpensive place to live in the city. An entire floor with from two to four high-ceilinged rooms and a couple of fireplaces could be rented for only thirty dollars a month in one of the old Village houses.

Writers and artists were drawn to this quiet oasis within the city. Tom Paine, Edgar Allan Poe, Willa Cather, Stephen Crane, O. Henry, and many other writers had come here to live at some time in their lives. These earlier figures had been isolated individuals; most of the regular residents were of foreign origin, largely Italian. But beginning around 1913, a flood of poets, writers, artists, reformers, young rebels of all types, came pouring into New York City and particularly, "because the rents were cheap," into the Village.

This movement was part of the great reaction against traditional beliefs. Young people wanted to break away from everything they thought the nineteenth century had stood for: Victorian morality, sentimental optimism, outworn conventions and taboos. They wanted reality, freedom, and self-expression. They did not know just what reality was or exactly what they wanted to express, but they were determined to find out for themselves. They rejected the definitions and rules laid down by their parents. They wanted to explore "the essential truth," following, perhaps, the new guideposts set up by Freud and Marx.

Some of the young people who gravitated to the Village came from small towns where money was the measure of success. A young man wanting to become a writer or artist or to pursue any of the non-money-making careers was considered something of a freak. In the Village he could be free from what he regarded as false values—he could live and dress simply and cheaply, devoting his main energies to writing, painting, or whatever else he wanted to do, without any loss of status.

Many of the residents of the Village were not in any sense artists. They were often white-collar workers, librarians, teachers, social workers,—anyone at all, in fact, who wanted a milieu where cultural rather than economic values prevailed, and where they could be free of the conventional restraints of the small towns from which they had fled. In the Village they could find a degree of privacy impossible in their home towns. As Edna Millay said in a letter to her family, "There is a beautiful anonymity about life in New York."

Among those rebelling against the old ways were young women who were discontented with the restrictions imposed upon their sex. They demanded independence and equal rights with men. They wanted to vote, to enter professions, to have careers outside the home. They wanted to be considered not just as feminine adjuncts to a masculine world but as individuals in their own right, with brains and abilities equivalent to those of men.

This was not an altogether new movement. Throughout the nineteenth century a small group of American women had fought for the right to control their own property and keep their own earnings, to go to college, to get the same pay for the same work as men. Most of all they fought for the vote, organizing themselves into a variety of suffragist groups.

By 1913 the movement had grown. More and more women wanted not only the vote but emancipation from a hundred other major and minor restrictions. Restless and energetic young girls talked of escaping the narrow limitations of a life confined to the kitchen and nursery. They wanted a larger, freer life even if they had to forego the traditional female role of domesticity to get it.

In their quest for the fuller life, many young women left their home towns and came to the Village. Here, perhaps, they could work and live as they wanted to. They could find jobs and careers which in their own towns were nonexistent or closed to women. They could explore new relationships between men and women, based on companionship and common interests rather than on the older, more restrictive courtship patterns.

In the Village, girls could dress more casually, appear in public places unchaperoned (this was still "not done" in many areas), even smoke in public. This was, after all, still the period when life was heavily overladen with taboos governing even the smallest details of feminine behavior. One woman was almost asked to leave a fashionable restaurant because she repaired her make-up at a table in full view of the other diners. Another, who had smoked in public, received an indignant letter accusing her of being "vulgar and immoral." Women were still required to wear stockings when swimming at some of the public beaches. In the Village many of these taboos were suspended while young women, as well as young men, tried to define the "true morality" which, they felt, had been stifled by convention.

There was still another reason for the exodus of the young: the lack of stimulation in their home towns. How was an aspiring artist to grow in his own field while living in the average small town? Where were the libraries, concerts, museums, galleries, theaters? Most of all, where were the "kindred spirits" sharing his own values and hopes, with whom he could spend an enriched life?

In the Village he could find the stimulation and companionship he had dreamed of. There was an atmosphere of hope and adventure, of bold experimentation in art and in living. Everything was possible, anything might happen. There was a new world to be made, and the young arrivals to the Village felt confident that they could help make it. Art, life, love, beauty—it was all there, waiting for them.

The Village swarmed with groups of every kind. Some were purely social. Their members met informally in each other's studio apartments to talk endlessly about every possible subject, overflowing from the few chairs onto the floor as the cigarette smoke thickened above their heads. Some revolved about favorite eating places, like Polly's Restaurant with its upstairs adjunct, the Liberal Club, whose motto was "A Meeting Place for Those Interested in New Ideas." Here the talk was also voluminous and varied but even more spirited, with voices being raised against the din of the player piano to whose pounding beat young couples were dancing. "Every night was party night."

Other groups had as their cohesive element the production of experimental plays or the publication of small literary or political magazines. "Little magazines" of every kind were constantly appearing; and though most of these collapsed after a brief career, they all provided encouraging outlets for new and unknown writers and their even newer ideas.

There were political groups and social reform groups, and small independent circles, and cliques of painters, sculptors, dancers, writers, and actors. But no matter what their center or purpose, they were all filled with an energetic exuberance and a rush of new points of view that were to burst upon an astonished country and to send ripples of influence even to the remote small

home towns from which the Villagers had originally
fled.

One of the liveliest groups grew up around a "little
theater" movement—a movement which already included the Washington Square Players, the Thimble
Theater, and the Neighborhood Playhouse. It started,
as so much in the Village did, in the most casual and
offhand manner, arising largely from the overflow of
creative imagination and energy of a group of young
people who had very little to do with the theater in the
first place. It is true that one of the later members of the
group was getting some good amateur experience in acting and playwriting at Vassar College at the time of the
group's inauguration, but Edna Millay had not yet appeared on the Village scene, though the stage was being
set for her.

One night in the summer of 1915 a group of Villagers
were sitting on the porch of a cottage in Provincetown
on Cape Cod, Massachusetts, an area that had become
their favorite summer resort. The cottage belonged to
George Cram Cook from Davenport, Iowa, one of the
restless midwesterners who had come to New York after
the customary stopover at Chicago. That night he talked
about the theater. He had been disappointed in the commercial theater of the day, which was imitative and
stereotyped, providing only the lightest kind of cream-
puff entertainment. The realism which had begun to
enter American poetry and which had appeared in fiction

and criticism much earlier, had not yet found its way onto the stage.

Some day, he said, he was going to establish a theater that would be unhampered by the concern for profits which afflicted the regular commercial theater. As he talked, it occurred to him that he might not have to wait until "some day." "Why don't we put on plays here?" he asked.

His friends were enthusiastic. For the rest of that summer they amused themselves by performing one-act plays written by members of the group. The first performance was given in a living room, but so many of the people summering in Provincetown wanted to see it that they took a deserted fish house standing on the end of an unused wharf belonging to one of their members and converted it into a playhouse. They installed wooden benches from an abandoned circus, draped a little stage with fishnets as a backdrop, and called it the Wharf Theater.

When they returned to Provincetown the next summer, 1916, they resumed at the Wharf Theater. But they needed new plays.

One day George Cook and his wife, Susan Glaspell, were walking along the main street of Provincetown. They met a friend who told them about a young man who had come up to Provincetown with him, the son of a famous actor. "He has a trunkful of plays," remarked the friend. "We don't need a trunkful," replied Susan Glaspell, "but tell your young friend to come to our house tonight and bring one of his plays."

The young man was Eugene O'Neill, and the play was *Bound East for Cardiff*. Someone else had to read it aloud because the author was too terrified to do it himself. It was immediately produced, with O'Neill, almost sick with stage-fright, acting the part of one of the seamen. It was a triumphant success: the old wharf shook with applause. Other O'Neill one-act plays were presented. Though plays by other writers were also produced, they were overshadowed by the work of this hollow-cheeked, gloomy, but intensely original young man who was perhaps the first American playwright to deal with inward thoughts, feelings, and moods instead of with purely external events.

At the end of the summer the group decided to continue its activities in the Village. George Cook found rooms in an old building on MacDougal Street which could be converted into a playhouse. By the fall of 1916 the Provincetown Players, as they came to be called, were ready to begin their first New York season.

Other Villagers joined them. Among them was Floyd Dell, who had been a close friend of Cook's back in Davenport. Floyd Dell, slightly built, with sensitive, ascetic features and a quizzical half-smile, "with a look of great delicacy" and diffidence, has often been called the representative man of his time and place. He was considered the embodiment of the Village of the pre-20's. Serious, analytical, and questioning, he was bent on exploring institutions and human relationships with an honesty and objectivity that characterized many of the young intellectuals of his period. He was a fluent and energetic conversationalist. From Davenport, Iowa, like other young midwestern writers, he had gone to Chicago and then, in 1913, moved on to New York and the Village, where he soon became managing editor of the *Masses* (not to be confused with the *New Masses*). It was a lively, iconoclastic Village magazine, cooperatively owned and published by its editors, a publication, as Floyd Dell described it, standing for "Fun, Truth, Beauty, Realism, Feminism, and Revolution."

Dell himself wrote book reviews, poems, short stories, sketches, and plays. He also began work on *Moon-Calf*, the first of a series of novels that would contain evocative descriptions of the life and ideas of the period.

Most of his plays were satirical one-act pieces written for informal presentation at the Liberal Club. He also designed the sets, painted the scenery, stage-managed the productions, and sometimes acted in them as well. He had been doing this for two years by the time George Cook brought the Provincetown Players to New York. It followed naturally that the first New York performance of the Provincetown should include *King Arthur's Socks* by Floyd Dell, and that other plays of his should appear regularly on their bills.

The Provincetown broke every theatrical canon, violated every tradition, often going to exaggerated and ridiculous extremes. But despite the wild experimentation and even wilder internal quarrels, the Provincetown became, for a few years at least, one of the most vital groups in the Village. It was the seedbed for many talents, some of which, in addition to O'Neill, would flower later in the lusher gardens of the uptown, professional theater.

In December, 1917, during the Provincetown's second New York season, Floyd Dell began preparations for his play, *The Angel Intrudes*. A girl was needed for the ingénue part. "In response to that call," wrote Dell later, "a slender little girl with red-gold hair came to the . . . theater, and read 'Annabelle's' lines. She looked her frivolous part to perfection, and read the lines so winningly that she was at once engaged—at a salary of nothing at all, that being our artistic custom. She left her name and address . . . and when she was gone we read the name and were puzzled, for it was 'Edna Millay.' We wondered if it could possibly be Edna St. Vincent Millay, the author of that beautiful and astonishing poem, 'Renascence.' . . ."

This was, in a sense, Edna Millay's official introduction not only to the Provincetown Players but to the Village and to the heart of its unique, pre-20's atmosphere. It was an atmosphere that in its unparalleled combination of gaiety, intellectual ferment, freshness, and honesty, was both the reflection and the stimulus of one of the most dynamic periods in America's intellectual history. And with the perfect timing that characterized so much of her life, Edna Millay arrived just as that phase of Village life was approaching its greatest fruition.

12.

Floyd Dell

When I was sixteen no more than a day,
April—May!
I met a young man in the flush of the noon.
May—June!

His step was light and his manner was gay,
April—May!
And he came from afar, by the dust on his shoon.
May—June!

—Floyd Dell.

THE rehearsals for *The Angel Intrudes* began. Edna was
receiving no money from the Provincetown, but she
thought the experience might lead to a paid acting job
on Broadway. In the meantime she hoped to support
herself by selling poems to magazines and by the sale of
her book. Norma found a job in a munitions factory;
with the entrance of the United States into World War
I in April, 1917, thousands of such jobs were suddenly
thrown open to women.

At the end of each rehearsal Norma would call for
Edna. After a few rehearsals one of the young men at
the Provincetown became attracted to Norma and began to squire them home. This was Charles Ellis, a

88

young painter who had come to the Provincetown to work on settings but, following the pattern of so many of the group, performed as actor, director, and stage designer as well.

Floyd found himself increasingly drawn to Edna, as so many young men were to feel themselves drawn. He hesitated to be alone with her, however, and their relationship continued on a rather stiffly formal basis. He was probably a little afraid of her. "She had," he wrote, "a charm that belonged to herself. A sort of Celtic magic seemed to emanate from her like a perfume. She seemed a little aloof from ordinary concerns. . . . I thought of the Snow Princess, whose kiss left splinters of ice in the hearts of the mortal men who loved her."

The Angel Intrudes was given right after Christmas, 1917, with Edna Millay giving "a delicious performance." From then on she was known as "the beautiful young actress at the Provincetown."

Floyd Dell finished another play, a comedy called *Sweet-and-Twenty*, and offered one of the parts to Edna. She asked him to read the play to her. He invited her to dinner and after dinner read the play aloud. Edna liked it and was pleased with her role. The play contained a song, "April—May," which she offered to set to music, saying she had composed melodies for several of her own poems.

She was now a regular member of the Provincetown group. When she and Norma wanted larger quarters, Floyd went room-hunting with her and helped her find a room at 139 Waverly Place, just a few doors from the house in which Edgar Allan Poe had once lived. It was an unheated place and during the winter was often icy cold. The fireplace, burning wood at ten cents a stick, offered only a small area of refuge. Edna often sat on the floor close to the fire when she wanted to write. She sent out her poems, received rejection slips, but went on writing. Money was scarce and there were times when meals consisted of hardly more than bread and tea.

One day Floyd took Edna and Norma to visit some friends, Max Eastman, the chief editor of the *Masses* and a member of the Provincetown Players, and Eugen Boissevain. Boissevain was a coffee importer, half Dutch and half Irish, a big, vital handsome man, with a zest for living. He had been married to Inez Milholland, the beautiful suffragist idol of Vassar, who had died a little over a year before. She had collapsed halfway through a lecture, and Eugen carried her back to their hotel where she died shortly afterward of pernicious anemia. Before she lost consciousness, she whispered to him, "You go on and live another life."

Now he was sharing an apartment with his close friend, Max Eastman. Both Eugen and Max were warm, friendly, hospitable men; but for some reason, on this particular occasion when Edna met Eugen for the first time, they were cold and decidedly not their usual selves, never dreaming how closely Edna was to become involved with Eugen's "second life." At the moment, Eugen and Edna stirred no interest in each other.

The friendship between Edna and Floyd Dell continued to develop until they discovered themselves in love.
He found her endearing, tender, exquisitely sweet and
devoted, an enchanting companion—but also remote,
lonely, unreachable, with an almost non-human quality
about her. She was, he wrote, ". . . at moments, a scared
little girl from Maine, and at other moments an austere
immortal. . . ."

Warm and loving as she could be, there nevertheless
seemed to be a point beyond which she would not or
could not go. "She wanted to be loved," wrote Floyd
Dell, "but was afraid of being in love." Whatever the
source of her fear, it soon drove her into a state of impatient irritability. The exchange of tender endearments
gave way to small bickerings, further aggravated by
flare-ups of jealousy and uncertainty on Floyd's part.
He felt that she was keeping some part of herself from
him, and began to question her, trying to fathom the
elusive quality that kept her, ultimately, so remote. She
parried him by saying, "Floyd, you ask too many questions. There are doors in my mind you mustn't try to
open."

She did not believe in analyzing one's deepest self
too closely. In "Journal," a long poem written many
years later, she was to ask:

> If I, making my awkward way
> Among my cluttered thoughts some day,
> The lost and ominous key should find

To the sealed chamber of my mind,
Would I the secret room explore
And, knowing what I know, know more?

She answers that such knowledge might only be destructive:

In which case, 'twould be fairly wise
To leave it lying where it lies.

She felt that it was especially dangerous to tinker with a creative personality. "Don't you think," she asked Floyd, "that our virtues as poets or artists may spring partly from the faults of our nature?" He wanted to understand himself and the world as fully as possible so that he could exercise conscious, intelligent control over his life, but Edna was opposed to such intense probing. She regarded it as an intrusion upon her inner privacy.

When she was not defending herself against his attempts to understand her, she was arguing with him about the nature of love. She said that sooner or later all love must end. This was to become one of the repeated themes of her poetry. It was almost as if she wanted love to end. Floyd, however, felt very differently. He believed that love could be enduring, and wanted her to marry him.

She refused. "I'm not the right girl to cook your meals and wash and iron your shirts, as a good wife should. It just wouldn't work out."

As they talked about marriage, Floyd realized that she

was probably afraid that by becoming a wife and mother, she might be less the poet. She wanted to devote herself exclusively to her poetry and did not want to "belong" to anyone except herself. She did not want to spend her energies on domestic affairs. In an interview given later in her life she said that she liked to have a house kept in perfect order, but if she had to "live in a mess, or live in a neat room and give up writing, I prefer the mess."

Floyd was thirty years old. He wanted a permanent love, marriage, children. To Edna these appeared as distractions at the beginning of an exciting career as a poet. She was restless, adventurous, fearful of being tied down by love or responsibility. At this very period, when Floyd Dell was offering her a life of rooted stability, she was writing lines like "Life is a quest and love a quarrel—" and

> *My heart is warm with the friends I make,*
> *And better friends I'll not be knowing;*
> *Yet there isn't a train I wouldn't take,*
> *No matter where it's going.*

The domestic idyll for which he was seeking must have seemed a positive threat to her poetry and to the kind of life she wanted.

There was another, even greater, danger in marriage. This lay in the possible success of marriage. She could always flee from a domesticity that made her unhappy; she had the courage and spirit for such a flight. But suppose she found that she *enjoyed* being a wife and mother, and that her dedication to the writing of poetry grew muted until her work faded into mediocrity as a result of receiving only the second best of her energies and concentration? Suppose she were to stop writing altogether? This was a chance she would not take. Her first book had been published and acclaimed. She was now a recognized, professional poet, a status she had worked hard for and would not relinquish if she could possibly help it.

Whether or not her fears were justified, whether or not it is possible for a woman to combine poetry and matrimony, whether or not she might have successfully and delicately balanced the familiar feminine seesaw of marriage and career, was at that moment of her life beside the point. The danger seemed real enough, and so her fears were real.

Echoes of this conflict appear in some of her poems. One sonnet rejects the demand that she put aside poetry for the sake of ordinary, domestic love. The divine obligation of creating an enduring poetry must not be neglected for the sake of a transient, human relationship:

> *Cherish you then the hope I shall forget*
> *At length, my lord, Pieria?—put away*
> *For your so passing sake, this mouth of clay,*
> *These mortal bones against my body set,*
> *For all the puny fever and frail sweat*
> *Of human love,—renounce for these, I say,*
> *The Singing Mountain's memory, and betray*

The silent lyre that hangs upon me yet?
Ah, but indeed, some day shall you awake,
Rather, from dreams of me, that at your side
So many nights, a lover and a bride,
But stern in my soul's chastity, have lain,
To walk the world forever for my sake,
And in each chamber find me gone again!

In another early sonnet she rebels against the conventional image of women as nonintellectual, purely domestic creatures:

Oh, oh, you will be sorry for that word!
Give back my book and take my kiss instead.
Was it my enemy or my friend I heard,
"What a big book for such a little head!"
Come, I will show you now my newest hat,
And you may watch me purse my mouth and prink!
Oh, I shall love you still, and all of that.
I never again shall tell you what I think.
I shall be sweet and crafty, soft and sly;
You will not catch me reading any more:
I shall be called a wife to pattern by;
And some day when you knock and push the door,
Some sane day, not too bright and not too stormy,
I shall be gone, and you may whistle for me.

Young feminists of the postwar era were to quote this sonnet as a rallying cry in their battle for equality. The coming of World War I had enabled women to emerge from their domestic confines into the jobs and careers (and the financial independence) made available by the departure of men to the battlefront. This had taken out of the realm of theory the big debates about the twentieth-century woman. These revolved around the issues of marriage versus a career, self-expression versus dedication to husband and children. Could a woman manage both a career and a home, or must she sacrifice one for the other? And was she capable of the same intellectual, artistic, physical—or whatever—efforts as men? For Edna Millay no debate was necessary. She had realized very early that she was the intellectual equal of men, and that nothing must be allowed to keep her from writing poetry.

But she was troubled by something more than the fear of having her poetry submerged by marriage. There was also a restlessness, an inner disturbance, perhaps an ultimate need to be solitary, that came increasingly between herself and Floyd Dell.

They quarreled; she grew impatient and even hostile, as though she were deliberately trying to hurt and humiliate him. "Vixen" was his term for her at such moments, a name which pleased her. What he called the "dreamlike enchantment" of their earlier days was being raveled away by bickering and misunderstanding. It was true that her good humor could be restored by some display of wit or feat of intellect which would arouse her admiration and response; but it is difficult for a young man to put on a continuous performance of intellectual pyrotechnics. Floyd resented the necessity for such an effort on his part. The time came when he had had enough and told her so.

She retorted: "You are free to go. I won't detain you."

It was all over, he thought. He went back to work on his unfinished novel, and Edna continued writing poetry and trying to get a foothold in the theater. She was given a role in a play to be put on by the Washington Square Players. This was a more professional group than the Provincetown and might prove a better steppingstone to Broadway. But shortly after the play went into rehearsal it was withdrawn. Her disappointment was so great that "she cried like a heartbroken child."

In April, 1918, Floyd Dell, as one of the editors of the *Masses,* was placed on trial, charged with violating the Sedition Act of 1917. The United States had entered World War I on April 6, 1917. Many of the editors of the *Masses* were socialists and pacifists, against war altogether. With their usual outspoken directness, they had strongly protested America's entry into this one. Such opposition was declared by the federal government a hindrance to the war effort and hence a violation of the Sedition Act. Floyd's own indictment had resulted from an article he had written defending the rights of conscientious objectors, though he was not one himself. The rights he demanded were shortly afterward granted but, ironically, the charge was still held against him and, with the other editors, he had to stand trial. The magazine itself had come to an end in October, 1917.

Edna was deeply concerned with the questions involved in the trial. She shared many of Floyd's political
and social beliefs. She felt that the war was "a special horror" and was discouraged about human nature. "Man
hasn't climbed up as far from the ape and the tiger and
the primeval slime as we had thought." Though up till
now practically none of her social or political ideas had
appeared in her poetry, they were nonetheless strong
and definite. She was instinctively opposed to injustice
and oppression, and was eventually to use her art as a
weapon against them.

Edna and Floyd had not been seeing each other, but
now she attended the trial, drawn by the issues and by
her sense of loyalty to a friend in difficulty. The jury
was out for two and a half days while the defendants and
their friends wandered through the courthouse corridor,
waiting. Edna bolstered their spirits and helped pass the
time by reciting poetry. At last the jury announced that
they were unable to agree on a verdict and the defendants
were dismissed until a new trial with a new jury could
be held.

One day Floyd Dell received an unexpected visitor
—an old friend from his Davenport and Chicago days,
Arthur Ficke, now Major Ficke, carrying dispatches
from General Pershing in France to the War Department
in Washington. Arthur asked him to arrange a meeting
with Edna Millay. Despite their long and friendly exchange of letters, they had never actually met.

Floyd brought Arthur to Waverly Place where Edna and Norma were living. Charles Ellis came over, too, and he and Floyd went out to a nearby French pastry shop and brought back food for a party. There was one very large pickle, which they passed around. When it came to Norma she held it up and said, "This pickle is a little loving cup."

Arthur was delighted with Norma's comment and repeated it, saying it was a good opening line for a sonnet. He proceeded to improvise one on the spot, writing it down on the cover of a pastry box. The opening lines ran:

> *This pickle is a little loving cup.*
> *I raise it to my lips, and where you kissed*
> *There lurks a certain sting that I have missed*
> *In nectars more laboriously put up.*

They were all impressed with Arthur's fluency and skill. Edna, in particular, found herself stirred. After the years when he had existed for her only through his letters, she now saw an extremely good-looking young man with an elegant and distinguished manner. She found him full of good talk and stimulating ideas, not only on poetry but about a great variety of subjects. Arthur, in his turn, was equally drawn to Edna; and, before the evening was over, it was clear that they were falling in love.

Arthur had only a few days to spend in New York and, after completing his mission in Washington, he returned to France. But the encounter, though brief, was long enough to touch them both with an intense emotion. Some of Arthur's finest poems were to be inspired by her.

Mrs. Millay came down from Maine to be with her daughters. They took an apartment on Charlton Street, and Mrs. Millay, thin, eager, and radiantly happy about Edna's achievements, entered into the life of the Village with as much enthusiasm as the girls. She wrote poetry, sewed costumes for the Provincetown, took part in one of the plays, and bobbed her hair when that startling fashion was introduced to America. When the term at Vassar ended, Kathleen joined them, and the presence of the three Millay girls, "each beautiful in her fashion, rocked the Village to its . . . base. . . . The Millay sisters were by all odds the most sought-after girls in the Village."

Norma was an extremely pretty blonde, taller than Edna, though resembling her a little; Kathleen was also tall, but with a dark Irish beauty, quite different from her sisters. With Edna, they formed a striking trio. During this Village period Edna began her lifelong friendship with Franklin P. Adams, the famous F.P.A. of The Conning Tower column which ran first in the old New York *Tribune* and later in the *World*. He was one of the earliest admirers of her poetry and helped spread her fame by frequent references to her work in his column. When he went to Italy and saw the paintings of Botticelli, he

remarked that they looked as though the Millay girls
had posed for them. Alexander Woollcott, who was with
him, said that Botticelli's "Primavera" should really have
been called "The Multiplication of the Millay Family."

Edna's appearance went through striking, chameleon
changes. No two people described her in the same way.
Unlike her sisters, she was very small, only five feet tall
and weighing a little over a hundred pounds, with a
slight, almost boyish figure. She had delicate, though
irregular, features and a long, lovely throat. She made
quick darting movements—some observers compared
her to a bird—but once settled she could remain absolutely immobile with a remote serenity, "like a chiseled
Buddha."

Her hair was red, but shot through with bronze and
gold so that it could appear everything from red-gold
to reddish brown. Her eyes were described as gray-
green, yellow-green, blue-green, even hazel. Her skin
was very white.

There were times when she appeared altogether unre-
markable and almost plain—what one man, meeting her
later in Paris, called *"une belle laide,"* an attractive plain
woman. But when something stirred her—an idea, an
emotion, a response—her mobile features grew animated,
a radiance illuminated the irregular planes of her face,
and before one's very eyes she would become transformed into a strikingly beautiful woman. It was then
that she became the perfect image of the legendary
poetess.

Her voice was melodious and vibrant and capable of great flexibility. She could make it sound like a child's, high and light, yet it would deepen quickly when she was serious. Her speech was precise and clear, with no hesitant pauses. There were times when she spoke with a mannered, self-conscious archness and even used the baby talk which appears in some of her letters. When she was angry she bit out her words at top speed. At times she spoke with a passionate, dramatic intensity that her listeners often found something of a strain.

When she was completely relaxed and surrounded by her own friends, she had an effervescent sense of fun and often looked and acted like an impudent, freckle-faced Irish gamin or a frivolous, flirtatious young girl with nothing more serious on her mind than the next dance. And yet there were also periods when she would withdraw into a deep inner concentration, become remote and aloof even to those closest to her.

At Village parties and in their apartment on Charlton Street, the three Millay girls would often sing three-part songs, as they had back in Maine, with Edna assuming a throaty baritone. Sometimes they would do a little song-and-dance skit. They harmonized perfectly, and their songs were often clever pieces of their own composition.

The reunited Millay household was as lively and active as it had been during their childhood in Maine. Lawrence Langner, founder of the Theatre Guild, wrote: "The three beautiful Millay girls were something of an institution in Greenwich Village, and swarms of young painters, writers and poets made pilgrimages to their apartment on the top floor, where the young ladies were chaperoned by their mother from Maine, a bright little birdlike lady. . . . Evenings at No. 25 Charlton Street were a perpetual soirée with Edna holding court in one room, Norma in another, and Kathleen in the third, while Mother Millay fluttered on guard over her fledglings, hopping from one room to another."

One of Edna's habits during these Village days was to take an extremely long time getting dressed for a date. Young men had to wait long after the appointed hour, impatiently or resignedly wondering what was keeping her or whether, as one of them put it, she was trying on one dress after another until she had put on every outfit she owned before deciding which to wear. It was not only on dates that she kept people waiting. Once she took part in the activities of a dramatic group called The Other Players. Edna used to provoke the director by coming an hour or two late to rehearsals, when she came at all, but her performance was done with such complete understanding of the role that he forgave her.

Money continued to be the perennial problem. The theater had failed as a source of income, and her poems brought rejections as often as they produced checks— and even when checks did come, they were too small to live on. She now turned her hand to writing humorous sketches and short stories. They were clever, satirical, and original; many of them expressed fresh, unconventional views of routine social attitudes and behavior.

She was able to sell them to *Ainslee's* Magazine and later to *Vanity Fair*. Since she considered them strictly bread-and-butter pieces, she refused to have them appear under her own name, and published them instead under the pseudonym of Nancy Boyd.

In September, 1918, the second *Masses* trial was called. Again Edna came to court and walked with Floyd up and down the corridor, reciting poems while they waited for the jury's verdict. And once again the jury was unable to reach any agreement, though this time there were many more in favor of acquittal.

One of the defendants in the second trial was John Reed, a large, wildly energetic young Villager of flamboyant enthusiasms. He was a poet, journalist, and war correspondent who tended to become deeply and personally involved with whatever he was working on at the moment. His exuberant escapades and effervescent personality led to his being called the Golden Boy of the Village, a soubriquet which later gave way to the name of Storm Boy, as his social and political ideas grew more radical and his actions more provocative.

He joined the staff of the *Masses*, but his activities there were interrupted by the outbreak of World War I, and he dashed off to Europe as a war correspondent. When the Russian Revolution erupted, he moved on to this newest scene of action and became a firsthand observer of the events he described in his book, *Ten Days That Shook the World*.

He returned from Russia in time for the second *Masses* trial. That same fall he received secret news from his contacts abroad that negotiations to end the war had started. This was a month before the actual Armistice. To celebrate these good tidings, even though they were not official, John Reed, Floyd Dell, and Edna Millay spent the night riding back and forth on the Staten Island ferry, and walking along the moonlit Staten Island shore. They took turns quoting poetry, and then John Reed began to talk about the wild adventures he had had in his life. Edna listened with growing fascination. As the dawn rose over New York Harbor, the small, redhaired girl gazed up at the big brawny hero of these fantastic tales and murmured, like Desdemona to Othello, "I love you for the dangers you have passed." John Reed had been called the Golden Boy of the Village, Edna Millay was becoming its Golden Girl, and it was somehow fitting that they be drawn to each other.

A month after the ferry ride the war came to an end, with an official Armistice and official celebrations. Within the next year John Reed returned to Russia, where he fell ill and died.

Once more Floyd Dell asked Edna to marry him. This time she consented. "It looks as though we can't give each other up," he said, and she agreed. "Shall I give you a ring?" he asked. She replied, "*I* will give *you* a ring."

But only a few weeks later they were disagreeing again about the nature of marriage. Floyd realized that if she did marry him there would never be any emotional surrender on her part. They could not have the kind of relationship he wanted, or if they did she would chafe at what she considered restrictions upon her personal liberty. Again they broke off and now, at last, it was really over. "We who had spoken so many words to each other said nothing at the end. There was nothing left to say."

Not long after this final parting, Floyd met and married a girl with whom he fulfilled his dream of a stable, happy family life. He and Edna remained friends, though they were never again really close. But he never forgot her; she had flashed into his life "like a meteor," and to have known her was "a tremendous enrichment of one's life. . . . It was something that one would always be glad to remember."

Edna's friendship with Floyd Dell had followed a course which was to be repeated with other young men. She would start out behaving with exquisite sweetness and romantic devotion. Gradually she would become irritable and difficult until the situation became intolerable. There would be a breakup. If they became reconciled, she would never rake up the past but would repeat the pattern as before: all sweet tenderness, then quarreling, then breakup again. If the young man asked her to marry him, her doubts and fears about marriage would be stirred and in the end she would reject him, gently but with finality.

When it was all over, Edna would be left with still

another reinforcement of her belief in the transience of love. Her reactions would vary—from an apparently cheerful acceptance of the inevitable to feelings of hurt and loss. All of these emotions—which would change and deepen as time went on—would be reflected in her work, producing some of the most spectacular love poems in the English language.

13.

Aria da Capo

. . . I know a game worth two of that!
Let's gather rocks, and build a wall between us;
And say that over there belongs to me,
And over here to you!

— *From* Aria da Capo.

AFTER the war ended, the mood of the Village and of America began to change. The ardent zeal for reforming and remaking the world—for creating the "golden age of the twentieth century"—was ebbing away in the disillusion and horror of the war's realities. In its wake came the postwar reaction that would reach its full flood during the 1920's.

Floyd Dell called 1919 "the year of great hopes and terrible disillusionments." Halfway through the year the hope engendered by the "war to end wars" evaporated with the disastrous Treaty of Versailles, which abandoned President Wilson's principle of self-determination of peoples. It arbitrarily chopped up old countries and reassembled them into untenable new shapes that laid the foundation for yet another war. The war which everyone had hoped was going "to make the world safe for Democracy" was soon to produce Mussolini,

108

Stalin, and Hitler; in the United States it had been followed by the anti-democratic Palmer Raids, and by the harsh suppression of the striking coal and steel workers. The hopes raised by the democratic revolution which overthrew the Russian Czar had been quickly deflated when the Communist minority seized control. In 1919 the brutal, bloody civil war between the Whites and the Reds was still horrifying the world. And the year reached its final crescendo of disillusionment when the United States Senate voted against joining the League of Nations, the idealistic organization which had been created by President Wilson himself.

There was still a strong spirit of rebellion among the young, but the emphasis was shifting. Instead of being *for* the full, free, rich new life which would emerge after the old traditional fetters had been broken, they were now simply *against* the old ideas, faiths, and traditions, with nothing to take their place. The war and the failures of the peace had exposed the hollowness of the old beliefs, and the new generation felt it was futile to look for new faiths which might only prove as meaningless as the old. Instead of wanting freedom *for* a better life, they were now demanding freedom *from* every kind of restraint.

In this passage from a positive to a negative outlook, idealism gave way to cynicism, and the broad social view shrank to a preoccupation with the purely individual. The serious young writers, artists, and social reformers of the earlier Village were now joined by a new and different crop of freedom-seekers. The newcomers were interested not so much in freedom for art's sake as in freedom for the individual's sake. Unlike the earlier Villagers, they were self-conscious and belligerent about their freedom. Some of them were so busy cultivating their individualism that they had little time left for the creative work they more or less pretended to be engaged in. The early, cheerful spontaneity of the Village was beginning to cloud over.

Against this shifting background Edna Millay continued to live as one of the "earlier" Villagers, writing and acting more seriously than ever. She wrote a great many poems and turned out stories and sketches under the name of Nancy Boyd. Most of her work that year appeared in *Ainslee's* Magazine. All during 1919 every issue contained one of her poems, and almost half the issues contained a Nancy Boyd piece as well. Her mother and Norma sometimes helped her; Norma collaborated with her on a few of the Boyd pieces.

Her connection with the theater widened to include an active interest in the organization of the new Theatre Guild which was being formed out of the old Washington Square Players. She appeared in their first production. Her chief theatrical activities, however, still centered around the Provincetown Playhouse. The 1918–19 season opened with a production of her own play, *The Princess Marries the Page*, with Edna as director as well as in the leading role.

Not only Edna but Norma and even, on single occasions, Kathleen and Mrs. Millay appeared on the Provincetown stage. One particular bill might well have been entitled "An Evening with the Millays," with Edna, Norma, and Cora each appearing in a different one-act play.

In November of that same year she finished her best and most famous play, *Aria da Capo*, a symbolic parable attacking war. It was produced by the Provincetown Players in December. She directed it herself, with Norma in the role of Columbine, and Charles Ellis, who also designed the sets and costumes, as one of the shepherds.

It was a beautifully and skillfully constructed little play, taking its name from the musical term indicating a song in three parts, of which the third part is a repetition of the first. The play follows this form, using two sets of characters and two moods. The senseless tragedy of war is poised against the empty, incongruous fripperies of an indifferent humanity which hastens to brush the horrors of war out of sight. The counterpoint between bitterness and frivolity is perfectly balanced; the contrast between the two sets of moods and characters is underlined by a marked difference in language—light and satirical in the first and third sections, reflective and weighted with undertones of doom and irony in the middle section which deals with the juggernaut of war and its final debacle.

This duality, this interplay of opposites, these quick transitions from gaiety to melancholy, were to become characteristic of Edna Millay, in her personal relationships as well as in her work. She would switch from high-spirited good humor to acerbity, from extreme generosity to a self-centered concern with her own driving needs. The myth that was shortly to crystallize would present her as a gay, flippant Villager singing bittersweet songs celebrating mainly herself and the difficulties of love, but there were depths and shadows in both her personality and work that were growing more defined. *Aria da Capo*, with its attack upon war and the deadly game of power politics, was clearly one evidence of this.

Coming as it did during the wave of pacifist and anti-war sentiment following the end of World War I, the play was an instant success. It was put on almost immediately by dozens of dramatic and literary groups throughout the country. It was translated into French and played in Paris. In March, 1920, it was printed in *Reedy's Mirror*, one of the leading literary publications of the period, issued in St. Louis.

In the months following these early appearances of her play, the amount of Edna's correspondence doubled. "I find myself suddenly famous," she wrote, and added that she found the experience exciting and stimulating. She was invited to give lectures and readings of her poetry before literary societies and made her first appearance as an after-dinner speaker at an affair given by the Society of Arts and Sciences.

Until this time she had been known as "the beautiful young actress at the Provincetown." Now, after the success of *Aria da Capo*, she was called "the promising young playwright." Almost immediately afterward, her poems began to appear so frequently and to attract such instant response that she was soon to be called "America's leading woman poet."

One of the most important appearances of her poetry was in March and April of 1920, when *Reedy's Mirror* published her first sonnet sequence. The twenty sonnets of this group were later distributed among several different books, but in the meantime they helped establish her early reputation as an exquisite craftsman in the sonnet form and as an exponent of some remarkable views on love.

Nothing quite like them had ever appeared in American verse before. They explored love from the woman's point of view, but with far less of the sighing sentimentality and romantic gloss of earlier women poets. Indeed, it is the woman, not the man, who insists that love is transient and cannot last.

There is little of the forlorn sorrow of the abandoned woman, or of the woes of unrequited love. If anyone is going to do any abandoning or unrequiting, it will be *she*, not *he*.

Male poets had written before this about the fickleness of women, but this was the first time a woman not only openly admitted her inconstancy—"Faithless am I save to love's self alone"—but insisted upon her right to be inconstant, even saying that she had more important things to do than devote herself entirely to love. She wants to remain "stern in my soul's chastity" so that she can carry out the real purpose of her life, which is the writing of poetry, not the selfless love for a man. This was a far cry from the traditional insistence that love is the dominant emotion in a woman's life.

In this group of sonnets she is quite unsentimental about love. She knows that lovers can bore or annoy each other:

> *Sometimes when I am wearied suddenly*
> *Of all the things that are the outward you,*

or question their love:

> *And wonder why I love you as I do,*

and that lovers can accept from the very outset the fact that their love, too, will die. This openly "modern" approach to love on the part of a woman poet was unprecedented. Women may have felt this way privately, but they had not put it into verse.

With the regular appearance of her poetry and the success of *Aria da Capo*, Edna was now one of the outstanding Villagers. She was constantly meeting new people and making new friends. One of these was Edmund Wilson, at that time on the editorial staff of *Vanity Fair*. He had heard of her "enchanting personality" and had read her poetry with great interest before he actually met her. In the spring of 1920 he was finally introduced to her at a party.

Vanity Fair was a magazine which provided an encouraging and much-needed market for many of the writers and artists of the 1920's. Frank Crowninshield,

its editor-in-chief, opened his columns to all the new
ideas and bright young talents of the era. In July, 1920,
the magazine began to publish a large part of Edna's
poetry and all of her Nancy Boyd pieces. Most of her
income came from the Nancy Boyd work, though in
May of that year her earnings were augmented by a
prize of one hundred dollars from *Poetry* for "The
Bean-Stalk."

In addition to Edmund Wilson, another member of
the *Vanity Fair* editorial staff, John Peale Bishop, fell
under the spell of their new contributor and before long,
to the irritation of Frank Crowninshield, both of his
promising young editors had fallen deeply in love with
the poetic star of the magazine. By this time almost
everyone was falling in love with Edna Millay. She had,
wrote Edmund Wilson, "an intoxicating effect on
people," exercising a spell on "all ages and both sexes."
Whenever she appeared in front of her house, the neighborhood children would crowd around her. At Village
parties she would sometimes sit alone in a corner of the
room, quiet and unnoticed. Then someone would ask her
to recite her poems, and she would begin in low, musical
tones. The room would grow quiet, and soon this hitherto
unobtrusive young woman would dominate the entire
group with the thrilling quality of her voice, the mag-
netism of her personality, and the beauty which now
transfigured her face.

Though the number of her admirers grew, her "over-
mastering passion," Wilson discovered, remained her
poetry. Into it she poured her emotions, creating verse

that was astonishing for its richness of feeling at a time when the frank expression of feeling was beginning to recede from American poetry.

Yet it would be wrong to imagine that Edna Millay was occupied exclusively with emotions or that she was a woman of all feeling and no thought, as some critics maintained. Edmund Wilson speaks of her "tough intellectual side," and Max Eastman says in *Great Companions:* "Edna had as clear, hard, alert and logical a mind as I have encountered in man or woman. She surprised me continually . . . with her large and accurate knowledge about many things. . . . She had . . . the instincts and discipline of a scholar."

It would be erroneous, too, to think of Edna Millay's early poetry as concerned almost exclusively with love, though many of her admirers of this period, particularly among the newly-emancipated young women, rarely looked beyond her love themes. But the other themes were there: an awareness of nature, a responsiveness to art and music, even a joy in abstractions like mathematics. The famous sonnet "Euclid alone has looked on Beauty bare" stands as a magnificent refutation of all the accusations leveled against her as being a one-subject, one-mood poet. It is a hymn to the beauty of structure and logic, to the kind of intensely satisfying resolutions which Bach revealed in music and Euclid in geometry.

One of her most persistent themes was the joy of life. "Renascence" was filled with the passionate desire to remain alive and embrace nature. Her first book of poetry contained two rapturous paeans to life, "God's

World" and "Afternoon on a Hill." Even though in later years the note of joy will become muted and less often sounded, the sense of affirmation will continue to run through her poetry.

It was perhaps this very intensity of her feeling for life that led her to another major theme, that of death. Throughout her work, it appears repeatedly: the death of a beloved person, the death of love, the death of a bird or an animal; there are even comments on her own eventual end.

One of her most eloquent poems is the "Elegy," the last of a group called "Memorial to D.C." These were written to a Vassar friend, Dorothy Coleman, who died of pneumonia in 1918. She had had a beautiful voice, which gave Edna her theme for the "Elegy." Most of the qualities of her dead friend, she says, will somehow be transmuted by the earth into some form that will continue to exist. It is not for these that she feels the greatest grief but for the sound of her voice which is lost forever:

> *But your voice . . . never the rushing*
> *Of a river underground,*
> *Not the rising of the wind*
> *In the trees before the rain,*
> *Not the woodcock's watery call,*
> *Not the note the white-throat utters,*
> *Not the feet of children pushing*
> *Yellow leaves along the gutters*
> *In the blue and bitter fall,*
> *Shall content my musing mind*

For the beauty of that sound
That in no new way at all
Ever will be heard again.

. . .

But the music of your talk
Never shall the chemistry
Of the secret earth restore.
All your lovely words are spoken.
Once the ivory box is broken,
Beats the golden bird no more.

Here again is the stress upon sound so characteristic of Edna Millay. Nothing, not the most beautiful sights or impressions, could transport her like sound. Her ear was finely attuned to music, to human voices, to all the natural sounds of the earth.

In her later books she was to add still other themes and venture more thoroughly into social and political questions. *Aria da Capo*, a frankly anti-war play, might be considered the first of her political pieces, and she had already shown concern over attacks on free speech when she attended the two *Masses* trials. Even this early she was already far from confining herself to a single subject. *Aria da Capo*, which certainly did not deal with romantic love, and the Twenty Sonnets published in *Reedy's Mirror*, with their broad range of emotion, were brilliant proofs of her growing depth and complexity, both as poet and woman.

14.

Figs and Thistles

Cut if you will, with Sleep's dull knife,
Each day to half its length, my friend,—
The years that Time takes off my life,
He'll take from off the other end!

—Collected Poems.

AT the beginning of the summer of 1920 the Millays gave up their apartment in New York and went to Cape Cod. They stayed in a small house on one of the Truro hills, ". . . a mile and a half only to the outside surfy sea, a lonesome beach where you never see anybody but sandpipers." They were back on the sea again, though the shores of Cape Cod are very different from those of Maine, with sand dunes instead of great mountains, and little pine woods instead of forests, and patches of scrub oak and wild beach plum instead of wide-flung meadows of flowers. The house was extremely simple, with no plumbing or electricity and not much furniture. But Cora Millay and her daughters invested it with their usual high spirits, their diversified talents, and their quite remarkable personalities.

One of Edna's friends had loaned them an ancient, wheezy phonograph, and Edna spent a good deal of

119

her time playing Beethoven's Fifth Symphony on it.
When she was not actually writing poems and Nancy
Boyd stories to the tune of the Fifth Symphony, she
would commit parts of it to memory until, by the end
of the summer, she could whistle almost the whole of it.
The Fifth Symphony, she wrote, ". . . answers all my
questions, the noble, mighty thing, it is 'green pastures
and still waters' to my soul. Indeed, without music I
should wish to die. Even poetry, Sweet Patron Muse
forgive me the words, is not what music is."

It was here in Truro that Edmund Wilson visited her
and asked her to marry him. She said she would think
about it. But in the end she did not marry him or any
of the other young men who were courting her. There
were so many that Wilson once told her they should
organize an alumni association.

Edna was still deeply engrossed in the problems of
writing and publishing her poetry, and still keeping away
from any permanent attachment that might interfere with
her work. She was ready to cut herself off from anything that would distract her from working, and decided
that when she returned to New York at the end of the
summer, she would take an apartment for herself instead
of sharing one as before with the rest of her family.

Before returning to the city, she spent three weeks in
the writers' and artists' colony at Woodstock, New York.
While there, she met "a handsome and perfidious Don
Giovanni of an Italian baritone," a member of the Metropolitan Opera Company, whose chief importance in

her life was that he taught her to speak Italian. Her facility in learning new languages was as great as it had been at Vassar. After only three weeks' exposure, she could read it "almost as easily as French, which is to say, almost as easily as English." She also had her hair bobbed for the first time, during this interval.

She came back to New York in September and found a one-and-a-half-room apartment at 77 West 12th Street. Another apartment right next to hers on the same floor was occupied by Kathleen, who quit Vassar abruptly in the middle of her junior year to try her hand at writing instead of continuing with her study of mathematics. Perhaps it had been unwise for Kathleen to attend the same college as Edna. It was almost inevitable that the younger girl, who also wanted to write poetry, should feel a sense of competition with the successful older sister; to follow in her shadow at school must have been irksome for a girl who was ambitious and high-spirited in her own right.

Edna decorated the apartment in a Chinese style. This, she explained in a letter to Witter Bynner, was her way of following him and Arthur Ficke to China, where they were at the time. They had left the previous spring for a long trip to the Orient, and she missed them deeply. "Where you used to be," she wrote, "there is a hole in the world. . . ." By this time she had realized the extent of her love for Arthur. "I love you, too, my dear," she wrote to him in October of that year, "and shall always, just as I did the first moment I saw you." The fact that she hardly ever saw him in no way diminished her feelings. As she herself wrote, "It doesn't matter at all that we never see each other. . . . We shall never escape from each other."

It was during this autumn of 1920 that she first met the English writer, Llewelyn Powys, who became a lifelong friend. Powys had come to New York earlier that summer and had read Edna Millay's poetry. Her lyrics "amazed and enchanted" him, and late that autumn he found someone who arranged an introduction to her. He found her "dainty with a daintiness that can only be compared with the daintiness of Queen Anne's lace. . . . It is true that I did detect in her look an April shadow of vanity, but below this self-conscious protection was a living representation of the divine spirit of poetry." A few years later he wrote a book, *The Verdict of Bridlegoose*, about this first visit to America, and dedicated it "to Edna St. Vincent Millay, A Leprechaun Among Poets."

The big event of that autumn was the appearance of one of her most popular books, *A Few Figs from Thistles*. This was a group of light, flippant poems which she had decided to publish separately, apart from her more serious work. The first edition consisted of a little paperback booklet bound in bright colors. The thousand copies which were printed were quickly sold out, and during the next two years at least five more editions were brought out, with extra poems added in two of them.

A Few Figs from Thistles established her reputation once and for all as "the poet laureate of the nineteen-twenties," as "the spokesman for the new woman," and as "the voice of rebellious youth." All over the country young people were soon quoting the poems. How could that defiant era resist such a book? The very first poem or "First Fig," the famous candle quatrain, starts off by repudiating the advice of the older generation to live sensibly and moderately:

> *My candle burns at both ends;*
> *It will not last the night;*
> *But ah, my foes, and oh, my friends—*
> *It gives a lovely light!*

The notes of the impermanence of love, of woman's fickleness, and of the new independence of women, which were struck in her first sequence of twenty sonnets, are sounded clearly throughout this book. Several of the sonnets from this first sequence were reprinted in *Figs*, including the one whose opening lines are almost the leitmotif of this whole aspect of her work:

> *Oh, think not I am faithful to a vow!*
> *Faithless am I save to love's self alone.*

It is the love itself which is important and which she celebrates, not the objects of that love. "What interests her," observed Edmund Wilson, "is seldom the people themselves, but her own emotions about them. . . ."

A variant of this idea is that love itself is always valid

and to be valued, despite its impermanence. In "Passer Mortuus Est," a poem composed at this time but published in her next book, *Second April,* she writes:

> *After all, my erstwhile dear,*
> *My no longer cherished,*
> *Need we say it was not love,*
> *Just because it perished?*

This was another new departure. Earlier generations had taken it almost for granted that a love which did not last had not, somehow, been a true love. But here was Edna Millay saying that a brief and fleeting love was just as real and true as any other.

There is a pertness, a saucy impudence—even a certain heartlessness—about many of these poems that people were to remember and associate with her long after these qualities had disappeared from her work:

> *And if I loved you Wednesday,*
> *Well, what is that to you?*
> *I do not love you Thursday—*
> *So much is true.*
>
> *And why you come complaining*
> *Is more than I can see.*
> *I loved you Wednesday,—yes—but what*
> *Is that to me?*

It was this audacity that found an immediate echo in the young rebels of the 1920's. Within a few months after its appearance *A Few Figs from Thistles* became the most quoted, the most mentioned, and the most imitated book in the United States. A whole wave of new light versifiers sprang up in its wake. Young people everywhere went around chanting, "My candle burns at both ends," until Edna herself probably became tired of hearing it. Samuel Hoffenstein, a contemporary writer of light verse, replied to it:

> *I burned my candle at both ends,*
> *And now have neither foes nor friends;*
> *For all the lovely light begotten,*
> *I'm paying now in feeling rotten.*

Books of humorous verse or parodies—a favorite form in the twenties—were hardly complete without a take-off on Edna St. Vincent Millay. Floyd Dell, traveling out to California shortly after the first edition of *Figs* came out, found people reading it all across the continent. She had become the most celebrated and talked-about poet of the day.

And yet, at the very point at which Edna was achieving her greatest popular success, at the very time when she was being hailed as the embodiment of the gay spirit of the Village and of the 20's, the gaiety was ebbing out of her own spirits.

Though her literary success should have seemed more assured than ever, she was running into some curious obstacles. Caroline Dow, to whom she felt deeply indebted, disapproved of some of the poetry Edna had been writing. *Figs* must have seemed the final affront to her. It was a painful situation for Edna. She wanted to avoid causing distress to Miss Dow, yet she felt even more strongly that she must not change even a comma simply to please someone. One of her deepest convictions was that she must never deviate from the truth as she saw it and as she felt impelled to write it. She refused to make any concessions in order to placate or curry favor with another person, even someone who had done as much for her as Caroline Dow. She once wrote a poem containing the line "A bucket of blood in my path." Floyd Dell and Arthur Ficke did not like the line and Arthur told her so. She replied: "I had rather give up a bucket of your blood, Arthur, than this bucket of blood."

Another difficulty facing her arose out of the publication of her second book of serious verse, *Second April*. She was letting Mitchell Kennerley, who had published her first volume, put out this one also. She finished reading proof on *Second April* early in April, 1920; the book was to have come out by the end of the month. But Kennerley ran into financial difficulties and kept delaying publication. Months passed with no word from him. From the end of May on, he broke off all communication with her, refusing to answer her letters or to speak to her over the phone, though she knew, as she wrote Witter Bynner, "he is so near the telephone all the time that I hear his breathing." She thought of suing, but

eventually things were straightened out, though the
book did not appear until late the following summer,
more than a year after the originally scheduled date.
Even then, she had the greatest difficulty collecting
royalties from Kennerley.

In addition to her worries over *Second April* and Miss
Dow (to whom she wanted to dedicate the book), her
formerly vibrant health began to fail. Two years earlier,
during that first exuberant year in the Village, she had
remarked happily to Floyd Dell: "I'm as strong as a
pony." But now her vitality seemed to flag and she had
several dragged-out bouts with illness. Her new apartment, like her first Village room, was badly heated, and
she seemed to suffer more from the cold than she had
done earlier. She tended to be rather careless of her
health, eating casually, keeping late hours, going out in
all sorts of weather. If she found a conversation or a
party stimulating, or became absorbed in working over
a poem, she would keep it up through the entire night.

Altogether, there seemed to be an increasing sense of
pressure, an element of nervous tension. Edmund Wilson
mentions this sense of strain and the fact that she never
appeared relaxed. "There was something of awful drama
about everything one did with Edna. . . ." he wrote.
Early in 1920 Edna had written to a friend that she was
having "a sort of nervous break-down" which interfered
with her work and plans; in October she wrote to Witter
Bynner that she was "sad so much of the time." In December she wrote to her mother saying that she had

had bronchitis and "another small nervous breakdown."
Floyd Dell summed it all up when he said that she seemed
to have an air of "doom."

What was this "doom"? Was it the sense of tragic or
melodramatic destiny which frequently afflicts young
poets, who feel themselves set apart from the ordinary
run of humanity? Or was it just the natural result of
her difficulties and of the irregular hours and prolonged
efforts involved in creative work? The strain is particularly great if a poet cannot support himself by his verse
but must divert part of his energies into earning a living.
The financial pressure must have been heavy for Edna,
who had no outside source of support. At one time she
even thought of finding a job in an office but then decided
that long hours of routine work might mean the end of
writing poetry altogether.

Perhaps the sense of doom or foreboding arose from
her conviction that all human relationships must inevitably come to an end, a theme which she treated with
defiant impudence in her early work, but which she was
to infuse with a troubled and more complex mood as
time went by. In *Second April* she is no longer casual
about the ending of love, an ending which often takes
somber forms not to be found in *Figs*. Sometimes it is
death, either real or anticipated or imagined, that ends
love. This is true of the gently melancholy "Elegy
Before Death" and of the sonnet, which she admitted
later was written to Arthur Ficke, that begins, "And
you as well must die, belovèd dust." In another sonnet

it is not death which brings love to an end but her discovery of the emptiness, not of love (love itself never loses its value or meaning to her), but of the lover. She finds the loved one to be

> . . . *just one other mound*
> *Of sand, whereon no green thing ever grew.*

It ends, "Once more I clasp,—and there is nothing there."

Whether love ends through death, abandonment, or disillusion, it always does end, implacably and unavoidably. She insists upon this over and over, through lyrical verses and brooding sonnets, in a variety of moods and degrees of intensity.

Why was she so convinced of the impermanence of love? Was it because of a deep distrust of men, a distrust which might have started when her father neglected his responsibilities to his family? Did she feel thereafter that it was in the nature of things for men to abandon women, or to fail them in some way; and was she afraid, then, that the men who professed to love her might in the end fail her, too?

Perhaps her haste to abandon men in her poetry was an echo of her determination to leave a man before he decided to leave her. Perhaps a certain scorn and heartlessness which appears in *A Few Figs from Thistles* was her expression—an unconscious expression possibly—of her resentment of men. She had grown up in a household of singularly independent women and no men. For all the friendliness which continued to exist between the girls and their father, nevertheless the glaring fact of his absence must have impressed itself upon the consciousness of so sentient a child as Edna.

Her sense of impermanence and impending loss was by no means confined to love. The theme of death runs all through her poetry. But it was not in any sense a fear of or what some of her critics considered an obsession with death. She herself called death a "Supreme Nuisance, an obstacle in the road of life, insurmountable and unskirtable. . . ." If she is obsessed with anything, it is with life.

Her chief emotion about death is resentment of a blind and irrational force that will so rudely cut off life. "Down, you mongrel, Death!" she says in one of her poems. She resents death so much that it is not enough for her to know that there is a constant cycle of rebirth in the world. In "The Death of Autumn" she concludes:

> . . . I know that Beauty must ail and die,
> And will be born again,—but ah, to see
> Beauty stiffened, staring up at the sky!
> Oh, Autumn! Autumn!—What is the Spring to me?

Significantly, one form of her defiance of death—or perhaps consolation in the face of it—is contained not in the hope of an ever-returning spring but in the possibility of having her work live on after her physical death. This is the theme of "The Poet and His Book" in *Second April*. She assures death that she will remain alive as long as her verses are read, and then goes on to plead with her possible future readers:

Stranger, pause and look;
From the dust of ages
Lift this little book,
Turn the tattered pages,
Read me, do not let me die!
Search the fading letters, finding
Steadfast in the broken binding
All that once was I!

Right now, however, at this moment of her life, it was evidently not enough for her to go on writing. Along with the sense of impending loss, there was a sense of restlessness, perhaps even of displacement. She had found New York a wonderfully open world after the limitations of Camden and the schoolgirl confinement of Vassar. But she never established the kind of rapport with the city that she instinctively felt with the country. She still tended to be frightened by New York. There were too many, too high buildings, too much noise and traffic, too many people.

In *Second April* there are many places in which she speaks of her weariness of the city. ". . . I am weary of words and people," she writes in "Exiled," "Sick of the city, wanting the sea . . ." In "The Bean-Stalk" she speaks of ". . . the cackle / Of the city . . ." and ". . . the little dirty city . . ."

The time was approaching when she would feel impelled to leave the city altogether. But where would she go? Did she really belong anywhere? Perhaps her uncertain mood at the end of 1920 can best be summed up in the very first poem of *Second April*, called "Spring." It begins

> *To what purpose, April, do you return again?*
> *Beauty is not enough.*

She sees the beauty of spring but insists that

> *Life in itself*
> *Is nothing,*
> *An empty cup, a flight of uncarpeted stairs.*
> *It is not enough that yearly, down this hill,*
> *April*
> *Comes like an idiot, babbling and strewing flowers.*

This is one of her rare expressions of despair with life itself. She may doubt the possibility of a permanent or perfect love, she may question the intelligence or justice of human beings, she may be skeptical of traditional values and conventions, she may resent and defy death, but she had always felt an intense, lyrical joy in life, and especially in its manifestation through nature. It was precisely this quality that was to distinguish her from the pessimistic, nihilistic poets of her own period whose voices were beginning to be heard in an ever-increasing chorus. For Edna Millay to sound this same note herself reveals the disturbance and change which had come over her at this time.

The Village, too, was continuing to change. The upheavals of the War were now finding expression in the

Jazz Age. "Flaming youth" was making its appearance; the flamboyant spree of the twenties was under way. In 1920 the formal passage of the Prohibition Amendment, which banned the commercial manufacture and sale of liquor, set off the era of speakeasies, hijacking gangsters, bootleg gin, and hip flasks. Skirts and hair became shorter. The "flapper" appeared, with her plucked eyebrows, brightly painted cupid's-bow mouth, and flesh-colored stockings rolled to just below her knee, scarcely meeting the skirt above.

Almost overnight, it seemed, the older values, traditions, and controls were liberalized. There was a great release of personal energy. This in turn was accompanied by a release of economic energy, and the Jazz Age was also the Age of the Great Boom. But there was more to the twenties than just energy, new views of personal conduct, and a revolt against restrictions; there was more than the postwar disillusion and cynicism ordinarily associated with the decade. There were also courage and generosity and the development of fresh ideas and taste. The twenties struck out boldly in new directions, approached life with high spirits, and recaptured the sense of adventure which had animated America in earlier days. It was a lively, exuberant, exciting time.

The Village, however, suffered. Rents and prices went up during the twenties. Restaurants, bookstores, art galleries, became artificially "quaint" and "picturesque" in order to lure uptowners and out-of-towners who could spend money freely. Sightseers spread through the Village destroying the precious peace and privacy which, together with the low rents, had drawn the original artists there in the first place.

As the Village grew, in a sense, more "Villagy," as the Edna Millay of *A Few Figs from Thistles* was increasingly hailed as the spokesman of the Village and of the new spirit of the 1920's, as the legends about her as an apostle of the "new freedom" began to take shape, she herself began to feel more estranged from it. She felt she could no longer function there successfully. In December, 1920, she decided to go to Paris. She felt she needed a change, a ". . . change of everything," she wrote her mother. ". . . My poetry . . . needs fresh grass to feed on. I am becoming sterile here. . . . Also, New York life is getting too congested for me,—too many people; I get no time to work."

In Europe she would be alone and able to concentrate on writing. Frank Crowninshield helped make the trip possible by agreeing to print in *Vanity Fair* a series of Nancy Boyd pieces. He wanted her to sign her own name to these, offering her more money if she would do so. But she refused. She did not want the Nancy Boyd pieces, light, incidental sketches written to make money, to be taken for her serious work.

She saved and scraped together whatever money she could and, characteristically, spent almost all of it for a good stateroom and bath. She prepared for her trip with the same concentration with which she had prepared for her examinations at Vassar, by reading everything about Paris she could lay hands on. She brushed up her college

French and practiced speaking it with those of her friends who also knew the language.

Just before she sailed, Frances Stout, one of her Vassar roommates, came to say good-bye. Frances had been tutoring some girls in French at the time, and brought with her, along with some turkey sandwiches, a book about Paris that she had been using for her pupils. Over the sandwiches Frances, at Edna's suggestion, used the book to quiz Edna about Paris and discovered that Edna had mastered practically everything about the city. She had memorized the map and knew the names and locations of streets, museums, railroad stations, even of hotels.

She sailed for France January 4, 1921, on the *Rochambeau*, leaving behind her brief theatrical career, her family, and a whole galaxy of suitors. Most of all, she was leaving the Village. Though she would be there again, briefly and intermittently, her Village days were over.

15.

Europe

I go out nearly every afternoon & walk miles & miles. It is so fascinating, when I once get started, that I can't stop.

From a letter to Norma, Paris, 1921.

WHEN Edna Millay sailed for France at the beginning of 1921, she was part of an exodus of young Americans who were going abroad as fast as they could raise the wherewithal. Once again there seemed to be an uncanny sense of timing about her action. She had written "Renascence" just as the poetic renaissance was starting; she had come to the Village while it was at the apex of its most brilliant period; had sought a theatrical career both as actress and playwright just as a new dramatic spirit was getting under way with the Provincetown Players; and had written poems celebrating the independence of women just as the suffragist movement had reached its climax and the emancipation of women was rushing forward with new impetus.

On Edna's part the timing was completely unconscious. She did not put herself deliberately in the vanguard of any movement. Her life was of itself in rhythm with the spirit of the time.

136

In 1921 everyone seemed to be going to Europe or was planning to go, or had only recently arrived. Sherwood Anderson, Ernest Hemingway, F. Scott Fitzgerald, and many others who were to become the literary leaders of their generation were on their way over. Gertrude Stein and Ezra Pound were already there. Many of them stayed in Paris, usually on the left bank of the Seine.

They went to Europe for motives very much like those which had driven an earlier generation of young American artists out of the small towns and villages into the larger centers of Chicago and New York and into Greenwich Village itself. They were curious and adventurous. They felt that in Europe they would find the stimulation, the rich cultural life, the creative freedom lacking in America. These were the days when the United States seemed to be filled with H. L. Mencken's "Booboisie," with "soulless materialists," and with a standardized atmosphere hostile to the creative life. The young artists, writers, and "creative personalities" wanted to escape from all this; after the Village the next point on the escape line appeared to be Europe.

Exciting new movements in art and literature were bubbling up abroad, particularly in Paris. Literary experimentation was going on under the spur of James Joyce, Gertrude Stein, T. S. Eliot, and Ezra Pound. "Little magazines" and equally little publishers and bookdealers, all of them encouraging new, unknown writers, clustered in Paris just as they had once sprung up in Greenwich Village. If anyone wanted to write, paint, think, or just live creatively (this last category covered a host of near-talented, would-be-creative, and just plain restless young people), the place to go in the 1920's was obviously Paris.

There was still another reason for the flight to Europe. The rate of exchange in the 1920's was immensely favorable to Americans. A dollar went much further on the left bank of the Seine than in New York, and as for countries like Germany and Austria, in the grip of a sky-rocketing inflation, a young American could live in comfort on an allowance that would condemn him to an unheated attic room back home.

As a final fillip to the wanderlust of the Americans, Europe had famous art galleries, great historical monuments, all the trimmings to a creative life lacking in the small towns of the American hinterland. The whole experience of Europe lay spread before the eager young American like a sumptuous but wonderfully inexpensive feast.

Edna's own interest was aroused more by the new trends in art and sculpture than by the literary experimentation. She went to galleries and exhibitions, and had dinner with Brancusi, one of the most modern of the new sculptors, in his studio. Like Robert Frost and Edwin Arlington Robinson, Edna Millay was singularly unaffected by the new departures in poetry going on all about her. The classical forms were perfectly suited to her literary needs, and she felt no impulse to discard them.

The innovations in poetry had begun shortly after the onset of the poetic renaissance and, in a sense, moved in and took it over. In London, before the first World War, a group of poets which included Ezra Pound, one of the first and eventually the most bitter of the expatriates, started the Imagist movement which proclaimed the creed of "pure" poetry. In 1914 the formidable Amy Lowell of Brookline, Massachusetts, heard of the group, went to London to join them, and maneuvered Ezra Pound out of the position of leadership, which she then took over.

The Imagists issued their own manual of rules: use the language of common speech, and always the *exact* word, not the merely decorative; create new rhythms to express the new moods of the day; allow absolute freedom in the choice of subject; deal not in vague poetic generalities but present an exact image (hence the name Imagist); present poetry which is hard, clear, and concentrated, not blurred or indefinite. They threw out meter and rhyme, substituting free verse and what they called "un-rhymed cadence."

New schools of poetry now began to follow each other in dizzying succession. A new one seemed to spring up every time a group could scrape together enough money to publish a magazine or anthology or issue a manifesto. Some of them discarded rhyme and meter to such an extent that their verse seemed hardly more than bits of prose broken up into short lines; others revolted against conventional typography and grammar; still others threw out all rational meaning, producing just a series of sensory impressions.

Edna Millay may have been amused by the experimental schools but she went on writing along the lines she had laid down earlier for herself, molding and adapting traditional, classic forms to her own lyrical purposes. She was unswervingly independent, in her art as in her life, and resisted all the contemporary pressures against traditionalism.

But though she did not succumb to the avant-garde movements swirling all around her, she could not help being stimulated by the atmosphere of literary battle in Paris. It was an immensely exciting period in an immensely exciting city, and nothing in America at the time could have substituted for the experience.

She had arrived in Paris with scarcely any money left. Friends helped her until checks began to arrive for the Nancy Boyd articles. Most of her writing during these early months in Europe consisted of articles and stories. One of the few poems she wrote was "The Ballad of the Harp-Weaver," for which she was soon to receive the Pulitzer Prize. It was dedicated to Cora Millay and in it Edna reveals a good deal of her feeling about her mother.

She spent much of her time looking at Paris and absorbing its atmosphere. Though people meeting her found her at first "almost morbidly shy," she made new friends and entered into the stimulating life of the Paris cafés of the 1920's, especially the Rotonde and the Dôme. She bought some beautiful Parisian clothes and went dancing with the young American men who were flocking into Paris. At first some of them hesitated to ask her to dance, thinking that the shy and serious young poetess could not possibly dance well. To their astonishment she was an admirably graceful and accomplished dancer, and jazz parties—"le jazz hot" had invaded Paris along with the young Americans—were added to the routine of her life in Paris.

Many of the young American writers and poets made a beeline for Edna, who by this time had achieved a considerable reputation for her poetry and whose striking appearance and wit made her an ideal companion. She met the Benét brothers, both poets, Edgar Lee Masters, Deems Taylor, F. Scott Fitzgerald and his wife Zelda, among scores of others. Scott Fitzgerald later became, like Edna, a symbol of the sparkle of the 1920's.

She had found her change, her fresh stimulation, her new milieu. Edna St. Vincent Millay, the volatile young girl from Maine, the Vassar student, the "beautiful young actress at the Provincetown," was now becoming transformed into the sophisticated cosmopolitan. None of these successive incarnations completely replaced the one before. They all remained, submerged at different levels perhaps, but ready to appear at a moment's evocation. The young girl, overwhelmed and "waylaid by Beauty," the impudent Village gamin, the exquisitely feminine woman, the tensely reflective, inwardly turned poet, the witty, "tough-minded" intellectual, the world-weary sophisticate, were never far removed from each other. She could sit languidly at a café table in Paris, slightly bored by the attentive young men paying court to her, and then go back to her hotel room to write her mother that she was "crazy with excitement" at the prospect of a trip to the French seashore. Paris was simply adding another dimension to an already highly faceted personality.

During the summer, while she was still in Paris, *Second April* was finally published after its long delay, and was an immediate success. The review in *Poetry* started off: "If I could only sound a fanfare in words! If I could get up on some high place and blow trumpets, and shout and wave my hands and throw my hat!" The book was welcomed by many of the admirers she had gained through *Figs*, but it also pleased many readers who had found *Figs* too "cute" or flip. There was nothing of this about *Second April;* it represented her most serious and thoughtful work.

This was a good publishing year for her. New editions of *A Few Figs from Thistles* continued to come out, and three of her plays, *The Lamp and the Bell, Two Slatterns and a King*, and *Aria da Capo* appeared, separately, as books.

In September Edna took a short trip to Normandy with several young painters and writers. She stayed mostly at Dieppe, where she not only noticed but took the trouble to learn the names of fifty-four wild flowers which she had never seen before. Then she crossed the Channel to England where she spent a few weeks in Hertfordshire.

At the moment she was writing no poetry at all. This was what she had planned—not to write poetry for a year. She had begun, she wrote to her mother, "to write in certain forms almost from habit," and felt it was time to stop for a while. Then, when she started again, her work would be "fresh, & possibly in a newer form."

In October she went to Rome where she spent about two months. Her chief reason for going, she said, was that since she had found how easy it was to get about the world, she would probably never stay in any one place for very long.

Back in the United States both Kathleen and Norma were now married, Kathleen to Howard Irving Young, a playwright, and Norma to Charles Ellis. This left herself, said Edna, "just about three months from being an old maid." Just before leaving America, she had told Edmund Wilson that she would be thirty any minute.

Arthur Ficke and Witter Bynner had, by this time, returned from the Orient to America. She missed Arthur more than ever, but somehow they could never arrange to be in the same place at the same time. ". . . it is wicked & useless,—" she wrote to him, "all these months & months apart from you, all these years. . . . I tell you I must see you again.—"

But Arthur remained in the United States, and Edna set off on a trip through Albania and Montenegro. She went by horseback, spending up to ten hours in the saddle on some days, though her entire training and experience with riding consisted of a half hour spent on a horse during her stay in Woodstock a year and a half before. At the end of the trip, she sailed across the Adriatic and returned to Rome.

By December her funds were depleted. The Albanian

jaunt had been expensive and hotel rates in Rome were high, so she moved on to Vienna, at that time one of the cheapest capitals in Europe for a foreigner to live in. Austria, which had been cut adrift from its vast prewar empire, was in the throes of political and economic upheaval. The currency was highly unstable: prices seemed to change day by day and sometimes even hour by hour. The steadily mounting inflation, disastrous to the Austrians, made it an economic haven for an impoverished American writer whose dollars, however few, were nevertheless stable. The country was uneasy, there was rioting in the streets, and gloom had replaced the former *Gemütlichkeit* for which the city had been famous. Edna was not happy in Vienna. She called it a ". . . grey city where there is never a shred of sunlight." Her room was dismal, facing out on nothing but a blank wall, so close that she felt it was flattened against her window "like a hand." The room was so dark that she had to keep the lights burning all day. The heavy, greasy food made her feel ill. She would have left, but she had no money for traveling. So she stayed on, lonely and altogether wretched.

Her wretchedness, however, did not arise entirely from her surroundings. For some time she had noticed a change in Arthur Ficke's letters and had guessed that he was falling in love with another girl. His first marriage had come to an end, but Edna knew that she and Arthur would never marry. In a letter to Witter Bynner she flatly states: ". . . I should not wish to marry Arthur, even if it were possible. . . ." Perhaps she felt that though they loved each other deeply, they were temperamentally un-suited to sharing the ordinary routines of day-to-day domestic life. Perhaps one or both of them felt that a marriage between two dedicated poets would compound their already difficult problems. Or perhaps it was simply that while Edna had been in New York, Arthur had been either in Paris or on the other side of the world in the Orient; then, when Arthur did return to New York, Edna was off in Europe. And while in New York he had met Gladys Brown, the young woman whom he would eventually marry.

Though Edna said she never wanted to marry Arthur, though she said in her letters that his falling in love with someone else "doesn't matter," nevertheless she must have been distressed. ". . . There's no denying that I love you, my dear," she wrote to him after he had told her about the other girl.

A curious episode now took place between Edna and Witter Bynner. In one of his letters Arthur mentioned a letter sent by Bynner to Edna. She never received it, but from Arthur's comments she gathered that in it Bynner had asked her to marry him. Her provisional answer to this provisional proposal was yes. She had known and loved Witter Bynner for a long time. ". . . You are bound in the memories of my childhood," she wrote to him.

He now asked her definitely, and she cabled back her definite "Yes." He planned to join her in Europe in the spring, but in the meantime a troubled correspondence took place. He was evidently upset by the fact that she still loved Arthur. She admitted that she did, but surely, she wrote, it was possible to love more than one person. ". . . One must be either undiscerning, or frightened, to love only one person, when the world is so full of gracious and noble spirits."

Arthur was opposed to the marriage. He felt they were approaching it in the wrong way and at the wrong time, with their minds cluttered by other emotions. He wrote a letter in duplicate, sending a copy to each of them explaining his views. He was not against the idea of their marrying, he explained, but wanted them to wait until they could communicate directly and openly with each other before considering it.

In the end Edna and Bynner decided against marriage. But they—together with Arthur—remained close friends for the rest of their lives.

There was also, during this first trip to Europe, the rumor of a young Frenchman with whom she fell deeply in love. But there were too many obstacles in the way of marriage and nothing came of this either.

In February, 1922, Edna moved on to Budapest and began making new plans, not for marriage but for bringing her mother to Europe. This was a project which gave her great satisfaction. People got married all the time, she wrote to Norma. "But not everybody, after the life we have had, can bring her mother to Europe." She had planned earlier to do this but her financial difficulties and the confusions attendant upon her proposed marriage had led her to postpone the trip. Then she heard from Norma that their mother had been ill and upset, and she determined that nothing should interfere now. Her finances were somewhat better, too. Arthur Ficke had sent her a check from his father when she was so desperately broke in Vienna, and she had started a novel, to be called *Hardigut*, for which she received a five hundred dollar advance. She was finishing another article for *Vanity Fair* and asked Frank Crowninshield to turn the payment for it, one hundred dollars, directly over to her mother, to help pay her passage abroad.

Cora Millay arrived in France, where Edna met her, in April and fitted easily into the life of Paris. Humorous and tolerant, she went everywhere with Edna, to the cafés, to the parties, to all the gatherings of the young literary and artistic set of the city, and everyone loved her. When Edna was not taking Cora around to her usual haunts, Cora would take Edna around to sights that Edna would probably never have gone to by herself. They saw more of Paris, Edna wrote to Norma, in five weeks than Edna had seen in five months by herself.

They spent the summer and fall in England, mostly in a little thatched cottage which they rented in Shillingstone, Dorset. Edna had been ill for several months and needed rest. She was having intestinal trouble, brought on, perhaps, by the bad food and general neglect of her health in Albania and postwar Vienna and Hungary. In Shillingstone she had her own little hut off in a field, away from the cottage, where she could be completely alone. She spent most of her days there, scarcely seeing any living thing except a few horses, cows, sheep, and occasionally a shepherd leading his flock across the downs. Mrs. Millay nursed her carefully, cooking special food which she carried down to the hut. Edna rested a great deal, using what little energy she had to work on her novel and on the Nancy Boyd pieces which had been supplying a good part of her income for almost two years.

While they were in England, Edna and Mrs. Millay took a few brief trips, some to London, one to Ramsay Abbey, the resting place of Cora's ancestors, and one to Cambridge where Edna caught sight of A. E. Housman, whose poetry she loved and with which her own has so often been compared. She did not speak to him but followed his tall, thin figure and cotton umbrella for about half a mile, until he turned in at Trinity College, of which he was a Fellow. Later, when he expressed his admiration for her work, she felt that Housman's praise was one of the highest tributes she could receive.

In December Edna and her mother went to the south of France, then to Italy—Cora Millay refused to go home without seeing Italy. At the beginning of 1923 they returned to America.

Some of her views about Europe might be gathered from a lighthearted poem published under the name of Nancy Boyd. The Italians, she says, are nice, but they refuse to heat their houses, are forever sobbing Puccini, and though the Romans no longer have lions to prey on

Christian flesh they have a supply of certain smaller carnivora. The Hungarians are nice, but "their native tongue is like a typewriter in the next room, and every word beginning with the shift-key," and "Their wines are too sweet." The French are nice: they wear the most charming frocks in the world, "they put all their cream into cheese," and "insist on serving the vegetables as if they were food." They are delightful because

> *They kiss in the cafés and dine on the sidewalks.*
>
> . . .
>
> *Their rudeness is more gracious than other people's courtesy.*
>
> *But they are afraid of the water.*
>
> . . .
>
> *And they bathe with an atomizer.*

They may be jolly,

> *But they have no ear drums.*
> *Paris is the loveliest city in the world.*
> *Until she opens her mouth.*

The English are nice, but not so nice as Americans.

> *No matter with whom they are dancing, they dance a solo.*
> *And no matter where they go, they remain at home.*
>
> . . .

> *The English are an amusing people.*
> *They are a tribe of shepherds, inhabiting a*
> *small island off the coast of France.*
> *They are a simple and genial folk.*
> *But they have one idiosyncrasy.*
> *They persist in referring to their island as*
> *if it were the mainland.*

In any European country the hotels are "hateful and irritating." There are no ash trays, wastebaskets, or soap in the rooms.

It is the Americans, with their open, generous natures, their impetuous recklessness, their cleanliness, who are the nicest people in the world:

> *I like Americans.*
> *They are so ridiculous.*
> *They are always risking their lives to save*
> *a minute.*
>
> . . .
>
> *They sell their bread hygienically wrapped.*
> *The Europeans sell it naked.*
> *They carry it under the arm.*
> *Drop it and pick it up.*
>
> . . .
>
> *I like Americans.*
> *They either shoot the whole nickel, or give*
> *up the bones.*
> *You may say what you will, they are the*
> *nicest people in the world.*

Of course, Nancy Boyd's opinions were not supposed to be Edna Millay's, though they admittedly had a good deal in common. After Edna's return from Europe, a volume of the Nancy Boyd pieces was published, called *Distressing Dialogues,* with a preface by Edna St. Vincent Millay. In the preface Edna writes that she was Nancy Boyd's earliest admirer. "I take pleasure in recommending to the public, these excellent small satires, from the pen of one in whose work I have a never-failing interest and delight."

We can take it, then, that Nancy's reflections do to some extent mirror Edna's.

16.

Eugen

It's wonderful to write to you, my dearest. It takes the sting out of almost anything. . . . It's amusing to think how entirely, totally, ABSOLUTELY different everything would be if you were in this chair beside me.— It makes me laugh, it's so funny that there could be such a difference.

—From a letter to Eugen Boissevain.

When Edna returned to America, she was tired and ill. She did scarcely any writing and abandoned her novel, *Hardigut*, for good. She took a small apartment on Waverly Place, in the same building as a friend, Esther Root, whom she had met in Paris. Right after her return Edna introduced Esther to Franklin P. Adams, whom Esther was later to marry. It was F. P. A. who described Edna at this period as having a "high bright gaiety," despite her illness, and being "full of eternal fragility."

Esther often spent weekends in Croton at the home of friends whom she and Edna had met abroad. They wanted her to bring Edna along, too, but Edna always refused. One weekend, however, early in spring, Esther was so insistent that she finally persuaded Edna to go with her.

At Croton, in the evening after dinner, the two men

152

who lived in the house across the road came over. Esther introduced them to Edna, not realizing that Edna had met Max Eastman and Eugen Boissevain some years before, when they were all living in the Village. Other neighbors, including Floyd Dell and his wife, dropped in and they began to play charades.

At their first meeting Eugen and Edna had aroused no interest in each other. On this night, however, they were paired off together during the game and proceeded to fall openly in love before the very eyes of the rest of the party. This time there were no doubts or hesitations in Edna's mind. On May 30 she wrote to her mother, ". . . I love him very much, & am going to marry him."

Eugen Jan Boissevain was an attractive combination of adventurousness and solidity. He was big, handsome, dynamic, athletically trained, vigorous, good-natured, and jovial, yet at the same time sensitive and imaginative. With no special talent himself—except a remarkable talent for enjoying life—he felt most at home with creative people or, as he put it, "great personalities." They, in turn, responded to his warmth and perceptiveness. He was born in Amsterdam. As a very young man he had visited the United States and liked it so much that he decided to return later and make it his permanent home. He never lost his Dutch accent, which his friends called "delectable." He called Edna "Aidna" or "Vincie."

Eugen's mother was Irish, the daughter of the Provost of Trinity College in Dublin. His father was the head of the *Algemeen Handelsblad*, Holland's leading newspaper.

His ancestors had been shipowners for generations; his immediate family had extensive interests in the East Indies. Eugen himself was an importer, dealing in sugar, coffee, and copra from Java.

He was twelve years older than Edna. His first wife, Inez Milholland, the suffragist leader, had died in 1916. If there was ever a man who could allay Edna's fears about marriage or about the effects of marriage on her poetry, it was Eugen. He believed completely in the independence and equality of women. His first wife had been an important leader of one aspect of the struggle for women's rights; now he had fallen in love again with a woman who was, in her own way, a leader of another aspect of that struggle. He felt strongly that if a wife was doing work of greater significance than her husband, that work must come first in his life as well as in hers. He said, "Anyone can buy and sell coffee. . . . But anyone cannot write poetry." He was prepared to devote himself to her work, to see that she remained free of any domestic routine that might interfere with it.

Once it was settled that they were to get married, Eugen immediately began taking care of Edna. He insisted that she get at the source of the illness that had been plaguing her for the past two years, and took her to a series of physicians. She was put on a strict regimen of rest and permitted to work only one hour a day. She saw practically no one—except Eugen.

On the morning of July 18, 1923, Edna and Eugen were married in Croton-on-Hudson. After the ceremony they drove to New York, where Edna entered a hospital for a serious intestinal operation. Arthur Ficke came to see her just before the operation. She looked up at him and said, "If I die now, I shall be immortal."

When she was able to leave the hospital, they went to live in Eugen's house in Croton-on-Hudson. In the fall they moved to a hotel on Washington Square in New York City. For several months Edna was able to do very little.

In November her new book, *The Harp-Weaver and Other Poems*, came out. When it was being prepared for the press, she was still so weak that Arthur Ficke had to correct the proofs for her.

The title poem had appeared earlier in a little booklet of its own, *The Ballad of the Harp-Weaver*. For this, for eight sonnets printed in *American Poetry 1922* (and later included in *The Harp-Weaver*), and for an expanded edition of *A Few Figs from Thistles*, Edna Millay was awarded the Pulitzer Prize for Poetry for the year 1922. It carried with it an award of a thousand dollars.

The Harp-Weaver contained some of the finest sonnets she had yet written. Many of them are on her familiar theme of the impermanence of love. But there is a change: once, she had taken love's inevitable transience more or less lightheartedly, but now she regrets its passing in one rueful poem after another. In the sonnet "Pity me not," she asks for pity not because love ends but because she cannot help suffering when it does end:

This have I known always: Love is no more
Than the wide blossom which the wind assails,
Than the great tide that treads the shifting shore,
Strewing fresh wreckage gathered in the gales:
Pity me that the heart is slow to learn
What the swift mind beholds at every turn.

There are, of course, other themes besides love in *The Harp-Weaver*. She writes about death and nature and restlessness and about her need for beauty—a need so great that she takes delight even in unlikely objects ordinarily overlooked or despised. In "Feast," she reveals the aching joy of wanting or striving as compared with the dull satiety of having:

I drank at every vine.
The last was like the first.
I came upon no wine
So wonderful as thirst.

And there is "The Ballad of the Harp-Weaver," written with her own mother in mind, with its melodious and haunting echoes of Irish balladry.

The volume was enthusiastically received. Her position as America's foremost lyric poet was now beyond dispute.

Edna was beginning to make money. She was determined to pay off all her old bills and those of her mother with money which she herself had earned. It was too bad, she wrote to Mrs. Millay, that she had not been able to do this before she got married because ". . . everybody thinks it is my rich husband who has done it, when in fact it is really I myself, every cent of it, with money that I made by writing. . . ."

At the beginning of January she and Eugen moved into 75½ Bedford Street, a narrow brick house only nine and a half feet wide, thirty feet deep, and three stories high. Almost immediately afterward, Edna left on a reading tour through the middle west. It was an exhausting trip. Sometimes she felt she was simply exposing herself and her poetry to the immediate stare of a curious public—to people who came "to see what I looked like." She tired easily and felt "sunk in a lethargy of boredom. . . ." She had to remind herself of the handsome fees she was receiving, fees which she needed in order to continue her project of paying off all her bills and helping her mother without any assistance from Eugen.

The trip came to an end at last, and she returned home to relax and bloom under Eugen's care. After a brief rest she set off on another trip—but not to read. This time Eugen was taking her on a long voyage to the Orient and then around the world. They were gone for the better part of a year, visiting the Hawaiian Islands, Japan, China, Java, Singapore, and India. It was a slow, relaxing voyage. In China they stopped off at Chefoo, a little village on the shore of the Yellow Sea, where they chartered a Chinese sailing junk with a crew consisting of a man and a boy, and spent their days sailing to small nearby islands where they would swim or picnic or just lie in the sun.

From the East they continued around the world, returning to New York in the fall of 1924.

But the city could no longer hold them. Edna had had her fill of cities. She wanted her own garden. Also, the tiny little house on Bedford Street was much too small for the comfort of so large a man as Eugen.

The following spring he bought a farm in Austerlitz, New York. They named it Steepletop, after the tall pink spires of the steeplebush plant with which the fields and meadows of the farm were covered.

The spring of 1925 was crowded for Edna. She was invited to recite her poetry at Bowdoin College which was celebrating the Centenary of Longfellow and Hawthorne; her reading was a success and was followed the next morning by an animated conference with a group of students. Tufts College gave her an honorary Doctor of Letters degree. In between these and other events, whenever they could find a minute to spare, she and Eugen were busy with plans for the farm. In June they finally moved to Steepletop, which from then on was to be their permanent home.

17.

Steepletop and Ragged Island

Here we are, in one of the loveliest places in the world. . . .

—From a letter, 1925.

STEEPLETOP was spread out over some seven hundred acres on the slopes of the Berkshires, overlooking the Lebanon Valley. A hill rose just above the house; mountains ringed the horizon; wide views were spread out beneath their own rolling meadows. The farm was three miles from the village of Austerlitz. A steeply ascending road curved up to a cluster of white frame buildings with gray roofs. The house itself, deeply surrounded by large trees, was an old farmhouse in good condition, which the Boissevains remodeled to suit their needs but without altering its essential simplicity. New heating and plumbing were installed, and walls removed to make larger rooms. A new wing and a garage were added, and later, a swimming pool and tennis court. A little cottage in a field away from the house was converted into a study for Edna.

They plunged into the wonderful frenzy of fixing up

159

the place. Edna worked so hard at such a variety of chores that she hardly knew whether she was "writing with a pen or with a screw-driver." For weeks they shared the house with carpenters, masons, plumbers, fifteen mischievous children whom they had hired as berry-pickers, and even a swarm of migrating honeybees.

They planned to run Steepletop as a working farm. It had originally been filled with berries of almost every kind, both wild and cultivated (or tame, as Eugen called them), and with fruit trees. With the help of Eugen's nephew, a professional landscape gardener, they restored as much of this as they could. Although everything had been running wild for many years, they were able to start off almost at once crating and selling berries. They set out flower and vegetable gardens. There were also animals on the farm—cows, sheep, horses, a pet black pig, and of course dogs.

The large oblong living room had windows on three sides and a brick fireplace. Edna always put out food for the birds on the sill of one of the windows and on the ground outside it, often getting up before dawn to do so. The birds came to know this and the window was soon filled with their brilliant, flashing, fluttering colors. "She runs a hotel for birds," Eugen told the writer Vincent Sheean, when he came to visit them at Steepletop. Sheean felt that Edna had a special and even mystical affinity for birds. They seemed, in his eyes, to hover around her with an air of particular kinship and communication; but Edna dismissed his ornithological *mystique* by explaining that the birds came to her simply because she fed them. Whatever the reason for the attraction, Edna knew a great deal about birds and took a particular interest in them. She had watched and named and studied them ever since her childhood, when she had gone on pre-dawn bird walks in the mountains around Camden. At Vassar she and Professor Haight had waited for hours in a swamp for the moment at dusk when the male woodcock would perform his courting dance. After she began living at Steepletop, she jotted down notes in a small *Bird Guide*, giving dates and comments on birds she had seen. Where the *Bird Guide* had called the note of the English sparrow harsh and discordant, Edna had written in the margin: "It's no such thing! It's a sweet sound, you old meanie! Just because you don't like them!" In answer to a request from Llewellyn Powys, she drew up a list of "Birds seen from windows of house at Steepletop today, May 13, 1938." The list contains the names of twenty birds seen that morning, five seen within the last few days, five which she had not seen but knew were on the farm, and seven heard that morning but not seen.

The living room, with its "bird window" at one end, was furnished like the rest of the house, simply and comfortably. The only unusual touches were two pianos and the exotic wall hangings and curios which they had collected on their travels. There was also a bronze bust of Sappho on a marble pedestal.

Just at the top of the stairs they installed the library or, as it was sometimes called, the poetry room. It contained volumes of poetry in English, French, German, Italian, Latin, and Greek and a large collection of reference books. On the walls were a portrait of Robinson Jeffers, the modern American poet whom Edna most admired, a pen sketch of Shelley, and two sailing charts of Penobscot Bay. There was also a large sign on which was printed in red letters the single word, SILENCE.

When the initial pandemonium of building and repairing had died down, they were able to settle into some kind of routine—although "settled" and "routine" were words scarcely applicable to the Boissevains at this time. There was always an element of drama in their lives, always unexpected moves, unpredictable turns of fortune or fancy which could send them flying off to another part of the world or into another dimension of living. There were periods of complete isolation—during their first winter at Steepletop they were snowbound for weeks. They had no telephone, and Eugen had to take a long hike on snowshoes in order to get their mail at Austerlitz. "Our house is an island in the snow," wrote Edna.

Then suddenly Edna might decide that she wanted to travel or see people, and Eugen would make almost instant arrangements. Sometimes they would stay in New York for a few weeks, going on a continuous round of parties, dances, theater, opera, and intensive shopping, after which they would again withdraw to the undisturbed solitude of Steepletop. The second winter after they bought the farm found them in New Mexico; other winters were spent in Europe, the Caribbean islands, Florida, California.

Occasionally they entertained at Steepletop, sometimes on a very large scale. In the summer of 1930 they gave an enormous three-day party for about fifty or sixty people. Arthur and Gladys Ficke had bought a house about fourteen miles from Steepletop in 1928, and two other friends had just built houses in the area. Between them the four houses were able to provide enough bedrooms for all the guests. For entertainment the Boissevains arranged to have a touring group of actors present a play on a stage set up in a natural amphitheatre near the house. Not that any planned entertainment was really needed— the effervescent spirits of the Boissevains and their guests would carry any party along.

These high spirits often led to lively impromptu performances when they had guests—Edna would suddenly perform a Japanese samurai dance using a grass sickle as a sword, or the conversation at the dinner table would take the form of an opera recitative. If Norma were present, the two sisters might sing a duet. Eugen had his own form of spontaneous and quick-witted hilarity. He was a superb host, thoughtful and courteous.

Edna devoted a great deal of her time to music. Whenever she was at the farm and not actively working on her poetry, she practiced for hours every day. She frequently played in quartets, with the other musicians coming over from a nearby music school in Hillsdale. One summer, when the school dormitories were crowded, two of the young string students were invited to stay at Steepletop. Eugen gave the boys an old jalopy called the Suicide Wagon in which to travel to the school and back. Edna often played trios with the boys, or a fourth would be invited in to form a quartet.

After the tennis court had been put in, tournaments were held. At the end of each one, there would be a dinner with champagne at which Eugen presented loving cups to the winners. Edna enjoyed tennis and played it well.

But most of the time they were alone at Steepletop, living at their own rhythm. In the daytime they relaxed in the most informal clothes; for dinner, however, they often dressed up in full regalia, though there were just the two of them present. Edna's working hours might assume almost any pattern. Usually she worked in her studio out in its lonely field, even in winter, with a blazing fire going in the little stove. Occasionally she would wake up in the middle of the night, reach for the pencil and notebook which lay on a table beside her bed, and work till dawn. There were notebooks—the hardbacked ten-cent variety were her favorite—and pencils all over the house.

Although the first draft of a poem might be written in what she called "fever and excitement," forming itself as if "conjured out of steam," it was always followed by a careful and deliberate process which she compared to a "painful kind of sculpture." She would analyze it word by word, chipping away at it, stripping it "until there is not a superfluous syllable, not a redundant sound." She could work for years on the same poem, putting it away for periods "until it is cold, and I get a critic's point of view . . . as if it weren't mine at all." Then, with a fresh viewpoint, she would take it out and chisel away some more, until it finally satisfied her most exigent standards.

Whenever she finished a book or a particular piece of work, she would be exhausted from the nervous intensity of her concentration. It was then that she would turn gratefully to her piano, finding it "a thrilling change, like taking a trip to the sea." Or Eugen would take her off somewhere, to another part of America or abroad. But even when they were away, she would think of Steepletop and wonder how her flowers were getting along. When it was time to return, she came happily and gratefully. Steepletop was her refuge, her haven, her abode of Silence.

Eugen took care of everything. He gave up his business to devote himself to Edna. He took care of all the business details connected with her publishing and reading activities, answered the telephone (whenever they had one), and handled the correspondence whenever they bothered with it at all. Sometimes weeks would go by when letters remained unread.

With the help of several men, he ran the farm. He also ran the house, hiring and supervising the servants, seeing to it that the place was properly cleaned, the laundry washed, and the food bought, cooked, and served. He planned the meals. "I don't want to know what I'm going to eat," Edna once said in an interview; "I want to go into my dining room as if it were a restaurant, and say, 'What a charming dinner.'"

They had difficulty with servants. Sometimes they had four working in the house; and then there would be a minor domestic upheaval and they would be left, often quite suddenly or with guests arriving, with none. When that happened, Eugen took over the housework and cooking himself. He was an excellent cook, and took the same robust joy in turning out good meals that he took in everything else.

During servantless interludes he prepared and carried Edna's breakfast up to her. He insisted upon relieving her of every kind of domestic responsibility, saying that a lyric poet must not have her sensitivity dulled by the routine details of housework. Even if she did not have to do any of the physical work herself, he was convinced that the fine edge of her imaginative perceptions would be blunted by having to make out shopping lists or superintending servants. The interruption of a telephone call or a domestic question might cause her creative intensity to evaporate. She could not, he felt, be both a housewife and a poet.

In Eugen's view the tradition that the management of a household must be the province of the wife was ridiculous. The automatic assumption that the husband's work must come first seemed to him nothing but an expression of male vanity. When they were first married, he decided that Edna's work was far more important than his, and from then on all his actions were determined by the question, "What is best for her?" Their lives were arranged to suit her purposes only. His work would make it necessary to live in the city; she felt she could not work in the city. So he gave up his work and they moved to the country. Managing the house would have eaten away at her time and mood, so he managed the house. "Her work is to write poetry," said Eugen, "not to run a house."

During the years when he shared an apartment with Max Eastman, Eugen had directed their bachelor establishment and no one had thought it extraordinary. Why shouldn't he direct his own household now, he asked, if it would free Edna for more important work? In fact, Edna used to say, "Eugen and I live like two bachelors." She had the same complete freedom that she had before marriage and without which she could not function. She had never, as she put it, "settled down." She did exactly as she pleased, when she pleased. "That's the only way in which I can live and be what I am."

Eugen responded instantly to every mood or whim of Edna's. When she needed diversion, he "made things happen." If she suddenly wanted to go for a walk through the woods or pick berries or go hunting or give a party or drive to New York or fly to the south of France, he would drop whatever he was doing and arrange to go with her.

When she was ready for work, he set up a protective wall wherever they might be. In one apartment which they rented for a prolonged stay in New York, he installed a system of flashing lights to replace the bells, so that the sound of ringing would not disturb the perfect quiet upon which she insisted.

Once in a while Edna would turn domestic for a brief period, and put on an amazing demonstration of her abilities. She would appear in old clothes, with a cloth wound around her head, and scrub or cook or work in the garden with a speed and energy that no one could keep up with. One spring they returned home after a trip to New York to find the house a complete mess after a three-month regimen of a particularly inadequate housekeeper. They got up at six every morning, or earlier, and while Eugen worked in the kitchen garden, Edna spent half the day cleaning the house and the rest working out of doors.

But once she was back at her writing, her domesticity had perforce to be abandoned and Eugen would again take charge. He watched over her constantly, fending off every onslaught against her time and energy. When she was resting or working, he saw to it that she remained undisturbed, even by their own guests. He carefully screened visitors, keeping out curious intruders, of which there were a great many as her reputation continued to grow. So many people tried to drop in unannounced that a sign was posted, "Visitors received only by appointment."

Eugen defended Edna not only against the world but against herself as well. He kept her from being overwhelmed by any of her own moods—whether of depression or withdrawal or doubt. When she became angry, he calmed her down. Edna's temper could rise to a dramatic height: she clenched her fists and the veins on her hands would grow taut; her speech poured out at express-train speed; her whole body trembled. Then Eugen would murmur, "Now, Aidna, now, Aidna—" and gentle her down, reassuring and soothing her until the storm of her fury had passed.

Eugen loved his job of watchdog, protector, and guardian of genius. He performed it deftly and graciously, with no loss of his own identity or dignity. If anyone were to call him Mr. Edna St. Vincent Millay, he would "burst into roars of laughter at the good joke." He felt that the finest and most productive thing he could do with his life was to devote it to "a person so great in mind, so beautiful in spirit and in person. . . ." He considered it a privilege to live with so stimulating and rare a personality. "Vincent and I may get into an interesting discussion at six in the morning and at noon we are still not dressed, still talking, tremendously excited by ideas. We read books together; we tramp about; she talks over a new poem with me. . . . Any day I may have an hour of extraordinary beauty. . . . And her mind is so acutely intelligent and powerful. All the things are in her which make one at peace again with the human race. . . ."

Just as Cora Millay had precisely fitted the role of mother to a poet, so Eugen now served as husband to one. Not one of the other men she had known and might have married could have coped as he did with the special needs of her volatile and often difficult temperament. When she wanted solitude, he held the world away from her. When she needed contact with people again, he took over as host and surrounded her with stimulating friends. He enveloped her not only with warmth and security and protection, but with a sense of importance. She was the star, the very center, of the special world he created for her. Under his careful guidance and control, that world orbited around her in time with the unique rhythm of her own personality.

Steepletop, for all its loveliness, had one serious drawback. It was not on the sea nor anywhere near it. Eugen loved the sea as much as Edna did; he had spent his childhood on the Dutch seacoast as she had spent hers on the coast of Maine. Both of them loved to sail boats. At Steepletop, miles from the coast, they read yachting magazines avidly and hung sailing charts on their walls.

Early in the summer of 1933 Edna and Eugen went to visit Esther Adams, who had a house on Bailey's Island in Maine. They rose before dawn one morning to watch the sunrise. At first there was nothing but the wide sea, but as the light grew, an island appeared on the horizon. They watched it take form, and then Edna said, "That's the most beautiful island I've ever seen. I want that island."

That island was Ragged Island, one of the loveliest, most distant, and least accessible of the entire group in lower Casco Bay. There was no electricity or plumbing, and no means of communication with the mainland. It had originally been called Rugged Island, and had been owned by Elijah Kellogg, a minister and writer who had come to the area in 1844 and later wrote a series of boy's stories using the island as a setting, calling it "Elm Island." His house was still standing. Ragged Island consisted of about fifty wild acres, surrounded by high rock ledges and with only one tiny harbor.

They bought the island and renovated the house which Kellogg had built. It was kept very simple. A few tables and chairs and some beds were all the furniture they needed. Most of their meals were eaten outdoors; lobsters trapped in their own waters by Eugen were boiled in a large iron pot outside the kitchen.

Here they were really withdrawn from the world. They spent some part of every year on their island, entirely alone, wrote Edna, "to gather driftwood, and haul our lobster-traps, and make fish-chowders, and sail, and read, and sit on the rocks. . . ." Sometimes Eugen would take a boat and go off to the mainland for supplies. Edna spent long hours in the water; Vincent Sheean, one of the rare visitors to Ragged Island, said she was apparently part mermaid.

The island, remote and cut off by water, was even more of a retreat than Steepletop. Edna could let herself drift away from the tensions and insistent pressures of the world; she could even escape, perhaps, from herself. In a poem called "Ragged Island," she writes of "Clean cliff going down as deep as clear water can reach;"

There, thought unbraids itself, and the mind becomes single.

There you row with tranquil oars, and the ocean
Shows no scar from the cutting of your placid keel;
Care becomes senseless there; pride and promotion
Remote; you only look; you scarcely feel.

Even adventure, with its vital uses,
Is aimless ardour now; and thrift is waste.

Oh, to be there, under the silent spruces,
Where the wide, quiet evening darkens without haste
Over a sea with death acquainted, yet forever chaste.

For all the winters abroad or in the south, for all the traveling and the intervals in New York City, her life from 1925 on was rooted in Steepletop and, later, in Ragged Island as well. Edna St. Vincent Millay, regarded by so many as the high priestess of the 1920's and the classic prototype of the Villager, had removed herself, right in the middle of her own decade, to another sphere altogether. To see her only as an urban figure of the 20's and only as the rebellious poet of *A Few Figs from Thistles*, is to view her fractionally and to miss the subtler overtones of both her personality and her poetry. In the solitude of her two retreats, she could penetrate layer after layer of her own mind and heart, down to where "thought unbraids itself." In the same way, her poetry responds to careful reading and rereading until the wider emotion coiled within the layers of lyrical cadence and imaginative phrase is fully communicated.

18.

The King's Henchman

The sight of thee
Is like a knife at the heart.
Of thee the sight or the sound,
The turn of thy head, thy speaking,
Is like a thing found,
To a man seeking.

—From The King's Henchman.

THE Metropolitan Opera Company wanted a good opera by an American, to be sung in English. Twelve American operas had been performed at the Metropolitan during its early history, but they were so inferior that the feeling had arisen that Americans were incapable of writing good opera and that English was an inadequate tongue for operatic singing.

No American opera had been produced by the Metropolitan since 1917, and native composers began to complain that they were being unfairly discriminated against. To refute this charge, the Metropolitan asked Deems Taylor, a young American composer and critic, to do an opera for them. He was commissioned early in 1925 and immediately quit his job as music critic on the New York *World* to compose it.

173

First, he needed a libretto and asked his friend Edna St. Vincent Millay to write one. She agreed. By the end of November she had written one act based on the story of Snow White and the Seven Dwarfs. Then she decided it wouldn't do and set to work on a completely different theme. This was based on a story taken out of the *Anglo-Saxon Chronicle*. It was half legendary, half historical, and to it Edna added an old legend of Allhallows Eve. It was set in tenth-century, Anglo-Saxon England before the Norman Conquest; she did careful research into the language of the period so that no English words of Norman or later origin appear in the text. It is written entirely in the rough, virile, heavily consonanted Anglo-Saxon speech, with scarcely a word that was not actually in use in tenth-century England. She also used a good deal of alliteration, as the old Saxon bards had done.

There were some people who thought that an American opera should be based on a strictly American subject. It was suggested that she use an Indian theme; but she felt that the Anglo-Saxons were much closer to us than the Indians were. The roots of our language were, after all, grounded in Anglo-Saxon, not in any of the Indian dialects.

The opera was written practically by correspondence. Deems Taylor and Edna saw each other only about four times during the entire period—about eleven months—before the final orchestration was completed.

Throughout that time Edna was suffering terribly from an almost continuous headache accompanied by "a veil of dancing dark spots" before her eyes. But despite the painful physical difficulties and the distractions of the remodeling operations going on at Steepletop, which they had recently bought, she worked steadily on the libretto, spending hours at a time in her little hut out in the fields. In the fall of 1926 she and Eugen went to New Mexico, where the libretto was finally completed.

The première of *The King's Henchman*, as it came to be called, was on February 17, 1927. The audience on that opening night was one of the most brilliant ever seen at the Metropolitan, with celebrities from every field. They received the opera with tremendous enthusiasm. Each act was followed by thunderous applause and shouts calling for the composer and librettist. At the end of the opera the ovation lasted twenty minutes.

Finally they stood alone on the stage, as one reporter described it, "the scholarly musician and the girlish, frail young poetess." There was a pause and then Edna said, "I thank you. I love you all." Deems hesitated a moment, then added, "That's just what I was going to say."

During the ovation the occupant of seat C-108 joined steadily in the applause. She was a small, thin, gray-haired woman who regarded the events of the evening with pleasure and satisfaction but without surprise. She had known all along that her daughter Edna—or Vincent, as she still called her—was perfectly capable of turning out a masterpiece, whether it was a sonnet or an opera libretto, and the enthusiastic acknowledgment which the audience was now according her was only to be expected.

Her other daughters were also doing well. Norma was singing in Mozart's opera, *La Finta Giardiniera*, which had opened at the Mayfair Theatre just a month earlier, and Kathleen had published her first novel, *Wayfarer*, the previous fall and was now preparing her first volume of poems, *The Evergreen Tree*. Mrs. Millay's three girls had amply lived up to their mother's belief in them.

Immediately after the première, newspaper and magazine reviews, articles, and editorials appeared, filled with praise for "the best American opera we have ever heard." It became front-page news. Both composer and librettist were credited with having swept away the barrier against American opera. One magazine writer said the opera had "killed forever the oft-repeated question, Is opera in English possible?" An editorial writer declared that *The King's Henchman* proved that "Uncle Sam can be just as sound artistically as he is financially. . . ."

It was given fourteen performances during the course of three seasons, a record for American opera at the Metropolitan. The second performance was given on February 21, four days after the first. The house was again sold out and again the work was given a tumultuous reception, with Edna and Deems Taylor coming out for repeated curtain calls after each act. The receipts for each evening came to more than fifteen thousand dollars. It was reported that, altogether, Edna received ten thousand dollars from *The King's Henchman*. The opera toured the country with the same spectacular success.

When *The King's Henchman* was put out in book

form (dedicated to Eugen Jan Boissevain) it was as successful as the performance. Three separate editions adding up to more than ten thousand copies were exhausted after twenty days, paying Edna royalties of a thousand dollars for just that period alone.

The King's Henchman was her second triumph as a dramatist—*Aria da Capo* had been the first—but the difficulties had been greater here because of the need to shape her work to fit another medium, the operatic stage. Her background in music had been of great value, as had the training in scholarly research at Vassar. Her success with *The King's Henchman* was an indication that she had become, as Lawrence Gilman put it in his review, "that young sovereign of the written word."

19.

"Justice Denied in Massachusetts"

*Let us abandon then our gardens and go home
And sit in the sitting-room.
Shall the larkspur blossom or the corn grow under this
cloud?*

—Collected Poems.

FROM the very start of her life as a poet, Edna Millay had been drawn to the social and political plight of man. She had expressed this as far back as "Renascence" when she called "All suffering mine," and in one of her first sonnets, "Not in this chamber only at my birth—," in which she identified herself as being a "child of all mothers" no matter what country or race. She called this sonnet, written in 1914 and inspired by the outbreak of World War I, the blueprint of her social consciousness. Later she had stood by Floyd Dell at the *Masses* trials, partly as a protest against encroachment upon freedom of the press. In *Aria da Capo* she had exposed the self-destructive folly of mankind and its irresistible drive to war.

Her concern with these issues, however, had always

178

been more or less generalized. In the 1920's an event took place that gave her thinking a specific focus. This was the celebrated Sacco-Vanzetti case. On April 15, 1920, in South Braintree, Massachusetts, a shoe factory paymaster, accompanied by a guard, was carrying a factory payroll of about sixteen thousand dollars. They were held up and killed by two men who made their escape in a car, carrying off the payroll with them. The police had no clues to the identity of the criminals, and there the matter rested.

Twenty days after the crime, in one of the routine roundups then taking place as part of the postwar raids against suspected radicals, two men, Nicola Sacco and Bartolomeo Vanzetti, were picked up as suspicious characters. They were Italians and anarchists, and were found with anarchist pamphlets in their possession. They spoke little English and were questioned through an interpreter, a procedure which caused confusion and misunderstanding. Although they had been arrested because of their possible anarchist associations, the authorities realized after the questioning that here were a couple of made-to-order suspects for the South Braintree murders.

They were tried and found guilty. The subsequent legal maneuvers, which took place during the next seven years, are a long complex of wrangles and blunders. Toward the end, however, several things became clear.

The men had been tried and convicted as much because they were foreigners, anarchists, and pacifists as because of any conclusive evidence of their guilt. The postwar public climate was hostile to anything foreign or in any way "radical"; even outspoken liberals were regarded with suspicion. William Allen White, the enlightened editor of *The Emporia Gazette*, wrote: ". . . every man who hopes for a better world is in danger of deportation by the attorney general." Some commentators had said that since the men were undesirable they should be executed, "whether or not they actually fired the shots. . . ."

The trial and the judge had been scandalously unfair. Judge Webster Thayer was singularly hostile to the defendants. Even those who were personally convinced of the guilt of the two men grew indignant at the bias of the judge and the inadequacy of the legal procedures. The Springfield *Republican* announced ". . . we are now forced to declare that a dog ought not be shot on the weight of the evidence brought out in the . . . trial of Sacco and Vanzetti."

Under the Massachusetts law of that period, it was the trial judge himself who ruled on appeals from his own verdicts. Later, and primarily as a result of the Sacco-Vanzetti case, the Massachusetts law was revised so that now, in a capital case, it is the Supreme Judicial Court which rules on new trials. But this reform came too late to help Sacco and Vanzetti.

And finally, during the slow, grinding years, there emerged the characters of the two men, revealing such gentleness and unworldliness that it became difficult to think them capable of committing a brutal murder. It also became plain that far from being "reds," as their accusers charged, they were, in Vanzetti's words, "opposed to every theory of authoritarian communism and socialism; for they would rivet more or less firmly the chains of coercion on human spirit. . . ."

All these factors, growing clearer as the years passed, brought about a reversal of opinion. Those who had doubted the guilt of the men were now convinced of their innocence. Those who had been sure of their guilt now had doubts. Many who were still unsympathetic to the men themselves were so disturbed by the unfairness of the trial and the bias of the judge that they felt the men had been unjustly convicted. Toward the end of 1926 the formerly hostile Boston *Herald* said in an editorial which was to win it the Pulitzer Prize: ". . . as months have merged into years and the great debate over this case has continued, our doubts have solidified slowly into convictions, and reluctantly we found ourselves compelled to reverse our original judgment." Many people felt that the death sentence should be commuted to life imprisonment as a form of insurance against the possibility of irrevocable error in case the men should later be proven innocent.

More and more people became agitated about the case. As the date of execution drew near, many writers and artists became involved in the effort to save the men. Among them were Edna and Kathleen Millay, Arthur Ficke, and Witter Bynner, all of whom wrote poems of protest. Impassioned articles and editorials were written, personal appeals were made. There was strong criticism from other countries. George Bernard Shaw and Albert Einstein wrote on behalf of the two men. In France one hundred lawyers drew up a legal protest against the verdict.

But in Boston itself there was little change. Judge Thayer remained adamant. For seven years motions for a new trial had been regularly presented to him and just as regularly denied. In April, 1927, he officially sentenced Sacco and Vanzetti to death. In August Governor Fuller of Massachusetts rejected an appeal for clemency. The final date set for execution, after several postponements, was August 23, 1927.

As the day drew closer, acts of protest were intensified both here and abroad. There were strikes and disturbances throughout the United States, and demonstrations against the American Embassies in several European capitals. The Ford plant in Argentina was bombed. There were riots in France and England.

On the morning of August 22 a few hundred sympathizers carrying placards began marching from the Defense Committee's headquarters in Boston to the Charlestown prison where Sacco and Vanzetti were being held. When the first group of paraders appeared in Boston Common, the police moved in on them and one officer shouted, "You are warned that you are violating the law! If you do not disperse, you will be arrested!" The paraders continued on their way. Two patrol wagons rolled up, and each marcher went down Beacon Street with a policeman gripping his or her arm. A second group appeared, were arrested, and removed. The third group consisted of thirteen writers and poets, headed by Edna St. Vincent Millay and John Dos Passos, one of the first writers to concern himself with the case. The same ritual took place: first the warning, then the patrol wagons, arrest, and removal.

Along with the others Edna Millay was taken to the police station and formally charged with violating the city ordinance against "sauntering and loitering." She was bailed out by Eugen, who had come up to Boston with her. He took no active part in the demonstration but put up bail for many of their friends.

That same day Edna obtained an audience with Governor Fuller. All day a stream of authors, editors, and lawyers had gone to plead with him. He received them courteously but insisted that he had to perform his duty, however unpleasant it might be. Edna urged him to consider the possibility of error. How could he be so convinced of the guilt of these two men, she asked him, when the whole world was in doubt? Where so many thoughtful citizens, although not in sympathy with the political opinions of these men, were convinced that the trial had been unfair, could he be so sure of his own judgment as to permit these executions in the face of the knowledge that human beings can often be wrong?

As an illustration of human fallibility, she told him the story she had heard as a child about the last hanging in Maine. Two men had been accused of murder. The evidence against them appeared conclusive, with nothing to uphold their own plea of innocence except the testimony of a simple fisherman. To many people this testimony constituted a reasonable doubt, but in the mind of the Governor of Maine there was not a shred of doubt. He refused clemency and the two men were executed. Some time later, on his deathbed, the man who had really committed the murder confessed. Surely, concluded Edna Millay, the Governor of Massachusetts, like the Governor of Maine, was but human flesh and spirit, and it is human to err.

Governor Fuller promised to think over what she had said. Edna left the State House, but later that day sent a letter reminding him of his promise. "Be for a moment alone with yourself," she wrote. "Look inward upon yourself." She concluded: "Exert the clemency which your high office affords. There is need in Massachusetts of a great man tonight. It is not yet too late for you to be that man."

That night everyone gathered in Salem Street, in the shadow of the Old North Church where the lanterns had been hung out for Paul Revere, and listened to Edna Millay read her poem, "Justice Denied in Massachusetts," which she had written about the Sacco-Vanzetti case. In it she talks about the blight that has come over the earth. The sweet, fertile land that we inherited "from the splendid dead" is overwhelmed by evil and has now become cold and sour. There is nothing to do but sit still, "Here in the sitting-room until we die."

A few minutes after midnight Sacco and Vanzetti were executed. When it was over, the crowd outside fell silent and then separated, some to walk the streets alone all night. In New York fifteen thousand people waiting in Union Square wept.

The next morning the men and women who had been arrested the day before in the "death-watch parade" were arraigned in court and fined five dollars each. All but six accepted the verdict, paid their fines, and were released. The six who refused had been selected to make a test case. One of them was Edna Millay. They pleaded not guilty, claiming that they had been exercising their lawful rights of peaceful persuasion and of expressing their views.

The police sergeant who made the arrest identified the defendants and the placards they had been carrying. When he pointed to Edna Millay and described the card that had been taken from her, she interrupted to say indignantly, "It was not that card!" The sergeant insisted it was. "The placard I carried," declared Edna, "had inscribed on it, 'If these men are executed, justice is dead in Massachusetts.'" The six were fined ten dollars apiece, but they announced that they would appeal, carrying the case if necessary to the State Supreme Court. "Anything," wrote Edna later, "to keep people from going to sleep on the subject." The trial was put off several times, and in the end they were acquitted.

There had been earlier arrests and trials for picketing. Dorothy Parker, whose poems were often mentioned as being in the same genre with *Figs from Thistles,* came out of the police station after her arrest rubbing her arm where an overzealous officer had gripped it. "Did they take your fingerprints?" she was asked by a friendly reporter. "No," she replied, "but they left theirs on me."

After Edna had seen Governor Fuller, she issued a statement containing her story about the last hanging in Maine. Shortly afterward a man who was studying Maine legal procedures wrote to the New York *World* pointing out several errors in her account. Other letters appeared in Maine newspapers declaring that both Edna and her attacker were wrong, and giving still different versions of the story. Cora Millay cut the letters from the Maine papers and sent them to Edna, who used the clippings as a basis for her own letter to the *World,* saying that though she had firmly believed her story to be the truth, she now realized that she had been mistaken. The first man who had corrected her was also mistaken. The man who had then corrected *him* had been mistaken. This succession of errors, all committed by people who were convinced that they were right, simply proved her point. "If in the very illustration which I used," she wrote, "I was myself in error, the force of my assertion is not lessened—that human beings with the best intentions in the world often made mistakes." She concluded that though Governor Fuller had been certain of his decision, it was not impossible that he, too, had made a mistake.

About two months after the execution Edna Millay wrote one of the few prose pieces to appear over her own

name. It was called "Fear," and was published in the
Outlook on November 9, 1927. Sacco and Vanzetti are
never once mentioned by name—she states that the reader
must be sick of names by now—but they are the un-
mistakable subjects of the article. It is a caustic analysis
of public hysteria, an emotion which she blames as the
primary cause of the executions. She accuses the American public of hypocrisy because it talks of justice but
does not exercise it. These men, she says, were put to
death because their speech and manners and ideas were
different from ours. Anything strange is regarded as evil;
an alien image is regarded with terror; differences are
considered dangers that must be done away with.

These men were anarchists, believing that man is so
essentially good that he does not require the control of
laws or governments. She cannot be an anarchist, she
says, for she cannot believe in the essential goodness of
man. Instead, she finds men filled with unreason and
cowardice and selfishness, with no capacity for love "beyond the love of a cat for the fire." The beauty of the
physical world, which once meant "all in all" to her,
can no longer make up to her "for the ugliness of man,
his cruelty, his greed, his lying face."

"Fear" aroused precisely the kind of hysterical response
that she castigates in the article. Vituperative letters
poured in to the editor of the *Outlook*, calling it a "vi-
cious, false, and wicked article," a "ludicrous piece of
nonsense." Her mistake about the last execution in Maine
had proved her point about the possibility of human

error. The reaction to "Fear" now proved her point about the existence of unreason in the United States.

For Edna Millay the whole experience was a head-on collision with injustice and mass hysteria. The impact reverberates through a good deal of her later poetry. The lighthearted gaiety which her early followers had considered the hallmark of her verse is shadowed by her disappointment and despair over the nature of man. In the sonnet sequence, "Epitaph for the Race of Man," published in 1934 in *Wine from These Grapes*, she shows how man triumphs over all the natural calamities of the world—wild beasts, earthquakes, volcanoes, floods, famines, fires—but is defeated in the end by his own greed and unkindness:

> *You shall achieve destruction where you stand,*
> *In intimate conflict, at your brother's hand.*

There is an echo of the theme of "Fear" when she speaks of man

> *. . . flinging a ribald stone*
> *At all endeavour alien to his own.*

In "My Spirit, Sore from Marching," which also appeared in *Wine from These Grapes*, she again expresses her disappointment in man:

> *Draw from the shapeless moment*
> *Such pattern as you can;*
> *And cleave henceforth to Beauty;*
> *Expect no more from man.*

This strain had appeared in her work before; it was by no means entirely the result of her participation in the Sacco-Vanzetti affair. Many years earlier *Aria da Capo* had exposed the self-destructive stupidity of mankind. But now her generalized concern with injustice and world problems had become channeled into specific cases and causes. These entered more and more into her poetry, especially as the spirit of the 1920's evaporated under the turbulent events of the 1930's and the approaching thunders of World War II.

20.

The Middle Years: Message to the World

Let me not shout into the world's great ear
Ere I have something for the world to hear.
Then let my message like an arrow dart
And pierce a way into the world's great heart.
—From an unpublished poem, written at about fifteen.

IMMEDIATELY after the climax of the Sacco-Vanzetti affair, Edna went on a reading tour. Throughout her lifetime she gave a great many public readings of her poetry, always with the same combination of preliminary dread and, once she had stepped out on the platform, assurance and even pleasure. She once said that during her tours she lived in a "continual state of anguish and terror"—"all nerves and headaches." When she actually found herself face to face with her audience, however, she would say anything that came into her head, feeling as comfortable and intimate with them "as if I were talking to one sympathetic person."

Her sense of theater, her background as an actress, her natural verve and style, contributed to the drama of her appearances. She dressed carefully for them, wearing long, flowing gowns in colors that set off her red-gold hair. She often wore green—one friend remembers vividly a green Fortuny gown—or prints with a green background, and usually a yellow or gold scarf which she held across her throat with her hand. She let her hair grow almost to her shoulders and while she read she would toss her head to throw her hair back, or lift her hand and push the hair back from her forehead.

During the course of a reading she would switch with great versatility from one personality to another. Sometimes she would sit in an imposing throne chair, speaking with intense dignity and solemnity; then she would become a young woman in love, with ecstasy in her voice and upon her enraptured face; then she would suddenly toss her head and, withdrawing the adult personality altogether, would read some of her poems about children, conveying the effect of an impish, freckle-faced little girl so convincingly that the audience would forget the long, formal, trailing gown and the high-heeled evening slippers. And then once again she would draw herself up and with her gown molding itself in long, straight Greek folds, would recite one of her sonnets with classic directness and simplicity.

Most of her listeners loved her and responded enthusiastically to the dramatic quality of her voice and personality. But there were some who felt that she read too slowly, losing the natural lyrical cadences of her own verse. Some found her too theatrical; others considered her too sentimental. There was an underlying beat of barely restrained emotion which some listeners found thrilling, but which to others seemed histrionic. She demanded perfect attention and complete silence from her audiences. After beginning one reading, she stopped and announced: "Unless those people who feel that they cannot restrain their coughing leave the hall, *I* am leaving."

Edna established a close personal rapport with her listeners and made special efforts on their behalf. Her 1924 tour took her to Minneapolis where she received a phone call from the Mother Superior of a convent in St. Paul. The nuns had been looking forward to hearing her, explained the Mother Superior, but since the reading in Minneapolis was scheduled for the evening, it would be impossible for the nuns to attend because the rules of the convent forbade their going out at night. Edna thereupon arranged to go to St. Paul and give a special reading within the convent itself. It was here that she met Sister Ste. Helene, Dean of the College of St. Catherine, with whom she established a warm friendship.

Her readings were always received with intense excitement, drawing overflow audiences wherever she appeared. Many of her devoted followers were perhaps as much intrigued by her personality as by her poetry, and were delighted to have the opportunity of seeing and hearing her in person. She received large fees for her appearances, but her traveling expenses were so high that she hardly considered the tours profitable. It was a far cry from the day in 1917 when she had written to Charlotte Babcock about her first paid reading: ". . . I was paid the fabulous sum of fifty dollars. . . ."

Eugen accompanied her on the tours, making all the arrangements and surrounding her with the comfort and reassurance without which she could not have endured the strain. She was tense and difficult—never knowing five minutes ahead of time what she wanted to do or eat or wear. Eugen helped her relax and practically barricaded their hotel suites to protect her from unwanted communication.

Even with Eugen's care, however, the tours were hectic and exhausting, with one reading following closely upon another. Occasionally they were interlaced with visits to friends who lived along the path of the itinerary or with hasty side-trips in search of diversion. On one tour to California the Boissevains stayed with a college friend of Edna's. During the week they were there, Edna gave five readings in four different towns. Into this crowded schedule they managed to squeeze a motor trip to Agua Caliente in Mexico for an evening of dancing, a visit to the writer Upton Sinclair, and two shopping excursions on which they bought four new evening dresses for Edna.

It was no wonder that she was worn out by the end of each tour. Eugen wanted her to cut down on the readings; but, despite the drawbacks of traveling, Edna enjoyed the immediate personal acclaim of her audience. Also, from time to time some special need for money arose. In a moment of extravagance, for example, she bought an outrageously expensive clown painting by Walt Kuhn and had to go on still another tour to pay for it, although she had previously turned down several offers in order to take life easy for a while.

In 1932 Edna added another form of communication with her widespread audience. This was through radio, which she believed had great potentialities for poetry. During the winter of 1932–33 she gave a series of Sunday evening readings over a nationwide hookup on the WJZ Blue Network. The broadcasts drew an unexpectedly large response. Enthusiastic letters came from all kinds of listeners and from all over the country—from oil drillers in Texas to West Point cadets—yet the radio executives had feared that the audience for such a program would be highly limited. The event had a special importance in American broadcasting. It was the first time that a literary figure had been given equal rating with stage and concert personalities.

One of Edna's close friends was Elinor Wylie, a poet and novelist famous for her delicately imaginative style. In 1921, while in Rome, Edna was asked to review Elinor Wylie's first book of verse, *Nets to Catch the Wind*. This was the only poetry review she was ever to write. Edna said the book marked the opening of "yet another door by which beauty may enter the world," and sent a letter to the author telling of her happiness at reading the poems. A year later the two poets were introduced to each other and a warm and intimate friendship developed.

Elinor Wylie had a sense of particular kinship with the poet Shelley, and the two young women often spent hours on such discussions as the relative emotional states of Keats and Shelley. To prove her points, Edna could quote page after page of either poet from memory. Whenever she had any kind of enforced leisure—when she was ill or traveling, for example—she would spend the time memorizing poetry, building up a storehouse of thousands of lines which she could quote at will.

In December, 1928, Edna was getting dressed to give the last reading of a long and exhausting tour at the Brooklyn Academy of Music. Someone who knew nothing about the friendship of the two poets mentioned casually that Elinor Wylie had died, suddenly, that very day. Edna walked out on the stage and began reciting, not her own poems, but those of Elinor Wylie.

During these middle years there were often guests staying at Steepletop. In the fall and early winter of 1930–31 the Boissevains turned their guest cottage over to Llewelyn Powys, the English author whom Edna had met back in her Village days, and his wife. At Steepletop Powys, already ailing with consumption, finished his book, *Impassioned Clay*, which he dedicated "To Eugen Boissevain, under whose roof and in the presence of whose daring spirit this book was finished." He enjoyed driving with Eugen in the horse-drawn sleigh during the frosty days, and crossing the snowy path to the Boissevains' fire-lit living room for pleasant evenings of conversation. In one of his letters Powys gives a complete census of the livestock on the farm at that time: two mares, two colts, two black working horses, Edna's riding horse named Rob Roy, four milking cows, seven heifers, one bull, one pig, one ram, four sheep, one large police dog, two small English setters, and one kitten. The Powyses left for the West Indies at the beginning of February.

On February 5, Cora Millay died suddenly in Camden and the world, wrote Edna, changed. "The presence of that absence is everywhere." Edna's relationship to her mother had been remarkable not only for the love which existed between them as mother and daughter, but for the regard in which these two rare women had held each other as individuals. Edna was not only filled with gratitude at her mother's encouragement of her as a poet—she had also adored her mother as a companion and admired her as a person of talent and courage. In 1921 Edna had written "The Ballad of the Harp-Weaver" as a tribute to the kind of unselfish and imaginative love displayed by Cora Millay to her children. After Mrs. Millay's death Edna wrote the group of poems, beginning with "Valentine," that were exquisite and poignant statements of her grief.

Though it was deep winter and heavy snow drifts covered the entire route, Edna had her mother brought from Maine to Steepletop, where she was buried.

In May of that same year, 1931, Edna Millay was listed among the ten greatest living women by John Haynes Holmes. Her sonnet sequence, *Fatal Interview*, dedicated to Elinor Wylie, appeared at the same time. It was hailed as her most mature work and her greatest achievement in the sonnet form.

And yet, with all her successes, there were periods when Edna felt depressed and helpless and ill. She suffered a great deal from poor health, and time after time some plan had to be abandoned or postponed because of an attack of flu or grippe. In a letter to Arthur Ficke she writes that life isn't one thing after another, it's the same thing over and over, ". . . first you get sick—then you get sicker—then you get not quite so sick—then you get hardly sick at all—then you get a little sicker—then you get a lot sicker. . . ."

Because of her fragile health they began to spend most of their winters abroad. In 1933 they went to the French Riviera. The following year they went to the Virgin Islands. Early in the spring they began moving slowly north, going from Puerto Rico to Haiti, Cuba, Florida, Charleston, then briefly to Steepletop, and from there to Ragged Island.

During this winter they heard that Llewelyn Powys was having difficulties. With three other persons, Powys had circulated a petition protesting the treatment of the inmates of a home for delinquent girls. They were charged with libel and, under the strict laws covering such cases in England at the time, were convicted and fined. Powys's fine and legal expenses came to almost three thousand dollars, a disastrous sum for him. When Edna heard about it, she immediately cabled him a thousand dollars, promised him another thousand in two weeks time and an offer of more if necessary.

She could easily spare the money during that period, as she wrote to Powys—her most recent book, *Wine from These Grapes*, had already sold more than forty thousand copies. But even when she could not readily spare it, she had only to hear of a friend needing money and she would send it at once.

The following winter (1935–36) found the Boissevains in Florida again. They spent about five months at Delray Beach where Eugen, going on ahead, had rented a furnished house. Edna came down with two of their servants on the first of December. At the beginning of May they went to Sanibel Island, off the west coast of Florida. Edna had with her the manuscript of a new book, *Conversation at Midnight*, on which she had been working for two years. Their luggage was sent up to their room at the Palms Hotel, and Edna went down to the beach to gather shells for her collection. A few minutes later she glanced back and saw the hotel go up in flames.

The building was completely destroyed. With it went all of her personal belongings—clothes, a favorite emerald ring, even the coat and hat in which she had traveled— and the manuscript of her book. When the shock of the fire had receded enough for her to think about it, she comforted herself by repeating a line of Catullus over and over, "Cease this folly . . . and what you see is lost set down as lost."

They drove miserably back to Steepletop with Edna

wrapped in a rug to replace the coat that had been burned. They looked so unpresentable, she wrote later, that they "slunk" into hotels late at night and "sneaked out before daybreak."

To add to her troubles, she had an accident in the summer of 1936 which was to give her years of almost constant pain and discomfort. She was sitting in their station wagon one night, and while it was going around a sharp curve, the door against which she was leaning opened. She was thrown out of the car and down a rocky embankment, rolling over several times before she was able to catch hold of a tree and stop. Her right arm and shoulder and several nerves in her back were badly injured, making it difficult and often impossible for her to play tennis or the piano, or to use a typewriter. Innumerable visits to an assortment of physicians and specialists, several operations, and a wide variety of treatments were to follow before she was able to get any relief.

She was plagued by illness. In December she went to New York City, planning to spend only a few days (partly to replenish the wardrobe that had been destroyed in the fire). She came down with the flu and had to remain. Other things came up and at the end of May she was still there.

During this stay in the city she received a letter from the Chancellor of New York University saying that the school wished to confer upon her the honorary degree of Doctor of Humane Letters, and inviting her to a dinner being given for a group of ladies by the Chancellor's wife. Edna accepted both the offer of the degree and the dinner invitation with pleasure. Immediately afterward, however, Eugen was asked to another dinner, to be given the same night as the ladies' dinner, at the Waldorf-Astoria in honor of the male recipients of honorary degrees. She was furious at this evidence of discrimination against women, and wrote a scathing letter to the Secretary of the University saying that had she known what was happening, she would have declined both the invitation to the all-ladies' dinner and the honorary degree. She objected to the whole situation, she wrote, not only for herself personally "but for all women," and hoped that she would be the last woman who would be asked "to swallow from the very cup of this honour, the gall of this humiliation."

Not only in her poetry but in the actions of her private life she was still demanding the full equality of women, still acting as the champion and defender of the rights that they had finally begun to win.

21.

The Middle Years:
The Poetry

How strange a thing is death, bringing to his knees,
*   bringing to his antlers*
The buck in the snow.
How strange a thing,—a mile away by now, it may be,
Under the heavy hemlocks that as the moments pass
Shift their loads a little, letting fall a feather of snow—
Life, looking out attentive from the eyes of the doe.
                                   —Collected Poems.

DESPITE all the distractions of these middle years, the time taken out for travel and reading tours, the time lost through illness, Edna continued to write and publish her poetry. In 1928 she published *The Buck in the Snow*, in 1929 *Poems Selected for Young People*, in 1931 *Fatal Interview*, in 1934 *Wine from These Grapes*, in 1937 *Conversation at Midnight*, in 1938 *Huntsman, What Quarry?* In addition to these, there appeared in 1936 a translation of Baudelaire's *Flowers of Evil*, done in collaboration with the poet George Dillon.

Though each of these books has its own quality, they are nevertheless distinguished as a group from her earlier

201

work. The youthfully buoyant assertion of life, the defiant resentment and repudiation of death, the gaily independent exploration of love have deepened in this later poetry into something subtler and more reflective. Death is now more than an unpleasant interloper and a supreme nuisance; in "The Buck in the Snow" she now says quietly, "How strange a thing is death. . . ." And in the same breath, she adds, perhaps even more quietly, how strange a thing is life.

The changes in her mood and attitude can be traced through the successive books. Before this, she had railed against death. Now, in "Moriturus" from *The Buck in the Snow*, she starts out by admitting that there might be some good in death—there might be peace. Heretofore, the search for peace had entered very little into her poetry —it was the action and movement, even the turmoil, of life that she craved. When she did search for peace it was in silence or in nature, rarely in death. Now she says that if in death she could retain some awareness of life,

> *If I could have*
> *Two things in one:*
> *The peace of the grave,*
> *And the light of the sun;*

then she might begin "To dicker with dying."

She quickly repudiates this kind of peace and returns to her old defiance. The short, tense verses rise climactically to her cry that any kind of living is preferable to the nothingness of death, and from there she goes to the final crescendo of her determination to resist death with the last of her strength.

In "Dirge Without Music," however, from the same volume, she knows that she must accept the fact of death though she still refuses to be resigned to it:

> *Down, down, down into the darkness of the grave*
> *Gently they go, the beautiful, the tender, the kind;*
> *Quietly they go, the intelligent, the witty, the brave.*
> *I know. But I do not approve. And I am not resigned.*

Later, in *Wine from These Grapes*, she finally admits that there might even be some purpose in the cycle of life and death. In "From a Train Window," she finds a grave-yard "by no means sad," but rather

> *. . . Precious*
> *In the early light, reassuring*
> *Is the grave-scarred hillside.*
> *As if after all, the earth might know what it is about.*

And in "The Leaf and the Tree" she asks,

> *When will you learn, my self, to be*
> *A dying leaf on a living tree?*

Here at last the continuity of life looms larger than the loss of a single individual.

But even with her changing view, she is not completely consoled. In "The Leaf and the Tree," though she recognizes that she herself is only a small and transient part of the human race, yet, she goes on to ask, just how enduring is the race itself? Is the tree really stronger than the leaf? Is it not in the end just as perishable?

> *The fluttering thoughts a leaf can think,*
> *That hears the wind and waits its turn,*
> *Have taught it all a tree can learn.*

She carries this question still further into two vigorous and caustic pieces in the same book, "Epitaph for the Race of Man" and "Apostrophe to Man." In these she suggests that the human race itself might die out altogether.

Nevertheless, despite her more thoughtful considerations of death, the inevitability of dying in no way diminishes the preciousness of life. This central belief of Edna Millay's beats as strongly and perhaps even more convincingly than ever throughout these books. Life must be held on to and savored at all costs. In "Lines for a Grave-Stone" she has a witty answer for those who feel driven by the wretchedness of their lives to welcome death. The man who has died addresses the living man who is complaining about his lot, and in the last of a series of incisive triplets, makes his offer:

> *Here lieth one who would resign*
> *Gladly his lot, to shoulder thine.*
> *Give me thy coat; get into mine.*

She once said to Franklin P. Adams that, like him, she was in love with life and wanted to live a thousand years. She agreed with him that it is better to have agonizing experiences than none at all, "for anything is better than nothing, and nothing could be worse than nothing." She believed that even "the worst was better than nothing."

There is also a ripening of her technical skill. She experiments with new and irregular verse forms, and introduces into many of the lyrics a longer and more flowing line, which she gracefully interweaves among the shorter ones. There are lovely fragments of imagery—a flower "utters her fragrance"; summer is gone, "Lost again like a shining fish from the hand," and

Beauty at such moments before me like a wild bright bird
Has been in the room, and eyed me, and let me come near
it.

There is a greater compression of meaning: she says more in fewer words, and the words are richer for the extra weight of the sense and emotion which they bear. Yet she manages to retain the simple and concrete language that had given her earliest work its startling freshness.

Among the best examples of this later work are "The Return," "My Spirit, Sore from Marching," and "Truce for a Moment." These poems also contain the clearest statement of her response to nature. In "The Return" the tone is restrained and objective, yet filled with tenderness. It begins:

> *Earth does not understand her child,*
> *Who from the loud gregarious town*
> *Returns, depleted and defiled,*
> *To the still woods, to fling him down.*

The particular kind of solace provided by an entirely impersonal nature is perfectly described in this poem:

> *But she is early up and out,*
> *To trim the year or strip its bones;*
> *She has no time to stand about*
> *Talking of him in undertones*
>
> *Who has no aim but to forget,*
> *Be left in peace, be lying thus*
> *For days, for years, for centuries yet,*
> *Unshaven and anonymous;*

Nature, to Edna Millay, is not an escape, or a storehouse from which to draw flowery adjectives to embellish a pretty verse. It does not provide symbols for philosophical or religious emotions. To this poet, who lived intimately with the manifestations of the earth, nature has a reality and significance entirely in terms of itself. She neither expects too much from nature nor invests it with qualities that appear in the romantic imagination rather than in nature itself. Nature and man exist in a state of harmonious balance. Earth is dispassionate; all creatures are alike to her. This idea is expressed in "The Return," and appears again in Sonnet IV of the "Epitaph for the Race of Man" in the same volume:

> *But no; you have not learned in all these years*
> *To tell the leopard and the newt apart;*
> *Man, with his singular laughter, his droll tears,*
> *His engines and his conscience and his art,*

Made but a simple sound upon your ears:
The patient beating of the animal heart.

Even when nature appears harsh or violent or cruel, it is never deliberately or personally malevolent. In the midst of a rough sea she can remain "snug and content . . ."

Because I knew that the sea
Was not concerned with me, might possibly
Drown me, but willed me no ill.

Nature is always detached and therefore, like beauty and unlike man, can always be trusted. In the trenchant quatrains of "My Spirit, Sore from Marching," she exposes the limitations and weaknesses of man—"Expect no more from him," she advises. Instead,

From cool and aimless Beauty
Your bread and comfort take,
Beauty, that made no promise,
And has no word to break;

In "Truce for a Moment" she presents an instant of perfect harmony in nature, a harmony which "Slackens the mind's allegiance to despair," and goes on to say in figures charged with subtleties of meaning,

For the duration, if the mind require it,
Trigged is the wheel of Time against the slope;
Infinite Space lies curved within the scope
Of the hand's cradle.

> *Thus between day and evening in the autumn,*
> *High in the west alone and burning bright,*
> *Venus has hung, the earliest riding-light*
> *In the calm harbour.*

For that single moment at dusk, the world and time and space, with all their fearful pressures, are checked and motionless. The early-rising Venus, the first star to appear in the autumn evening skies, shines like a ship's light indicating the quiet harbor in which the mind floats, suspended and, however briefly, at peace.

There is a difference in her love poems, too, in these books. The inevitable impermanence of love is no longer treated frivolously or with a simple, nostalgic regret. Disappointment and disillusion have become too keenly felt to be lightly dismissed. Many of these poems, like "The Cameo" and "Not So Far as the Forest" with their melancholy images of imperfect love, are intensely poignant.

The best of the love poems are contained in the fifty-two sonnets of *Fatal Interview.* Many readers have tried to find some reflection of her personal life in this love-sequence, but this is futile as well as irrelevant. Every poet bases his work upon his own emotions and experiences, but these are rarely transmitted directly into his work. They are the raw materials from which to draw upon, and during the creative process they are so reshaped that though the basic emotion or idea might remain unaltered, the details emerge in a new context bearing little resemblance to the original event.

In a sequence like *Fatal Interview*, the sonnets may have been woven together out of a series of unconnected experiences, or out of a broad range of emotions connected with no specific experience at all. Or they may have started as a group of unrelated pieces which were then fashioned into a continuous and unified exposition of the course of love.

Each of the superbly written sonnets describes another stage or incident in the development of a relationship; and, more significantly, explores another aspect of the complex emotions involved in love, particularly from the woman's point of view. This view has deepened over the years; love is now entirely serious and even tragic.

Unlike the early sonnets, it is the woman who seeks the love in the first place; and though she still believes that love must inevitably end, it will be the man who tires of love while she aches for it to continue. She no longer holds aloof from a complete surrender of her emotions but, against all advice and the lessons of her own experience, openly proclaims her love and offers it freely, even before there are any signs that it will be returned.

The sonnets are filled with the anguish of an unequally shared emotion—in which one person suffers the burden of loving or feeling more than the other. And yet, despite the anguish caused by love, despite its fleeting passage, it remains the supreme emotion and experience of life, for which no sacrifice is too great:

> *Heart, have no pity on this house of bone:*
> *Shake it with dancing, break it down with joy.*

> *No man holds mortgage on it; it is your own;*
> *To give, to sell at auction, to destroy.*

One of the most beautiful descriptions of what love can mean is contained in Sonnet XXX which begins,

> *Love is not all: it is not meat nor drink*
> *Nor slumber nor a roof against the rain;*
> *Nor yet a floating spar to men that sink*
> *And rise and sink and rise and sink again;*

and goes on to her central theme:

> *Yet many a man is making friends with death*
> *Even as I speak, for lack of love alone.*
> *It well may be that in a difficult hour,*
> *Pinned down by pain and moaning for release,*
> *Or nagged by want past resolution's power,*
> *I might be driven to sell your love for peace,*
> *Or trade the memory of this night for food.*
> *It well may be. I do not think I would.*

At the very height of their love, in another of the most moving sonnets, she has a moment of hope that love might be permanent after all. Long after they are gone,

> *When we that wore the myrtle wear the dust,*
> *And years of darkness cover up our eyes,*

she pleads

> *Tease not our ghosts with slander, pause not there*
> *To say that love is false and soon grows cold,*

But pass in silence the mute grave of two
Who lived and died believing love was true.

This is perhaps the first time in Edna Millay's poetry that there appears the possibility and belief that love— not the abstract emotion but a specific love between two individuals—might endure permanently. When the relationship does end, it is because the man's love wanes, while hers remains as strong as ever. There are several remarkably imaged sonnets which, almost like a delicate seismograph of the emotions, register the impact upon a woman of the loss of love.

Despite her own distress, there are no reproaches. The lack of rancor toward the departing lover and her refusal to employ dishonesty or guile in the service of love are all expressed in the sonnet beginning "Well, I have lost you; and I lost you fairly." She says

If I had loved you less or played you slyly
I might have held you for a summer more,

but she refuses to hold on to love once it has begun to falter, preferring to relinquish it voluntarily, without recrimination or regret. Love cannot be forced or held captive; it comes and goes at will and must be allowed to do so.

The last of the fifty-two sonnets, "Oh, sleep forever in the Latmian cave," is the only one written in the third person, and serves as a formal coda to the entire composition. As a final surprising note, there is an implication in the last couplet that human love, though the supreme emotion, has been in the end almost too filled with pain and anguish for one to bear.

In *Fatal Interview*, the defiant independence, the courage, the still remarkable fact that it is a woman, not a man, writing with such candor about love—all these have remained constant. But the sense of tragedy, of doom, which had hovered only like a faint and occasional aura over the work of the early days, has settled into a permanent framework, enriching and, indeed, ennobling her later work.

After the original manuscript of *Conversation at Midnight* was destroyed by the hotel fire in Florida, Edna Millay almost immediately set about rewriting it. With her excellent memory she was able to recall those sections which had been completed, but the unfinished ones proved nerve-wrackingly difficult. She later claimed that the restored version was not nearly as good as the original. She had had to reconstruct some passages and omit others, producing what she considered a "patchy and jerky" result.

The rewritten work was published in 1937. It reflected the great social and economic questions agitating the world during the 1930's. The grueling depression and the political experiments of communism in Russia and fascism in Italy and Germany had caused many people to examine our own democratic institutions more closely than ever. In *Conversation at Midnight* these questions—as well as war, religion, love, and a variety of lesser subjects—are presented by the device of bringing together seven men of different occupations and attitudes for an evening of talk. By the end of the evening a whole range of contemporary opinion, in all its diversity and conflict, has been exposed to view. No definite conclusions are reached. The author's own point of view seems to be most closely allied with that of the liberal who admits that he has no well-defined solutions for the world's ills. He knows only that he wants to eliminate poverty and injustice, but unlike the totalitarians with their highly organized systems, he does not want to achieve his goals at the expense of individual freedom and dignity.

Conversation at Midnight may lack the whiplash eloquence of her regular lyrical work, but it displays a remarkable awareness of political issues and a considerable dexterity in defining them. It is a significant stage in her passage to a wider concern with the external problems of the world—a concern which would soon fill her entire horizon.

Another evidence of her versatility was the translation of Baudelaire's *Les Fleurs du Mal* on which she collaborated with George Dillon. Originally she had been asked just to write the introduction to the book. She agreed, and he sent her some translated poems to look at. To compare one of Dillon's versions with the original, she picked up a copy of Baudelaire. A line from another poem caught her eye and, to her horror, before she could stop herself, she found that she had translated it.

This was a fatal and irrevocable step. Despite her struggles against it, she ended by becoming a full collaborator on the book. She embarked upon a meticulous and scholarly procedure, discussing difficult or obscure points with several professors of French and Latin. In the fall of 1935 she went to France to visit the little town of Honfleur in Normandy, where Baudelaire had been born. Some of the oldest inhabitants had seen him as a boy and were able to give her information to use in connection with the biographical notes for the book. Altogether, she put in eight months of hard, sustained work. When it was finished, she said, "Now I will have an absolute rest from all this," and by way of relaxation reread almost all of Vergil.

There was an interesting by-product of the undertaking. In the letters written to George Dillon and to some of the professors whom she consulted, and in the introduction to the book itself, she goes into an analysis of poetic technique and of the art of translating that constitutes one of the few written accounts of her ideas on poetry. She reveals herself as a careful technician, with a sound knowledge of the problems involved. In her introduction she talks of the inexorable relationship between the form and content of a poem, between its physical character, "its rhythm, its rhyme, its music, the way it looks on the page," and what it says. When the "suddenly quieted and intensely agitated" poet first conceives of his poem, she says, "its shadowy bulk is already dimly outlined."

The amusing letters to her publisher and to Dillon describe the trials of getting a book through the press, especially when complicated by geographical separation. During much of the working period, she was in Florida, Dillon in Virginia, and the publisher in New York. At one point, exasperated with the unreasonable actions of the publisher in not supplying enough page proofs to the authors, she suggests to Dillon that instead of returning the edited page proofs, they send in a corrected copy of the Bronx and Queens telephone directory and take off for the Galapagos Islands. She is witty, caustic, and acute, revealing an energetic temperament in these letters that is as striking as the emotions expressed in her poetry.

This temperament emerges from all her letters. She always claimed that writing them was extremely difficult for her, insisting that she suffered from an anti-letter-writing disease for which she invented the name epistola-phobia. They nevertheless read absorbingly. In the collection published after her death, they are by turns lively, sad, tender, sharp, self-critical, sensitive; above all they are intensely sincere and moving. For all their occasional air of lightness, some of it girlishly cute, there emerges the portrait of a serious artist who, as a woman, threw herself into life fully and generously.

22.

The New Poetry

This book, when I am dead, will be
A little faint perfume of me.
People who knew me well will say,
"She really used to think that way."

—Collected Poems.

It was clear that Edna Millay's work was developing constantly—becoming more flexible, acquiring greater breadth of theme and vision, gaining maturity of outlook —but what of her reputation? In the early 1920's her work had probably been more read and quoted than that of any living American poet. To most young moderns, wrote *Time* Magazine, "poetry meant simply Edna St. Vincent Millay." Her literary personality, said a contemporary poet, "completely filled the scene . . . . the name of Edna St. Vincent Millay was a definition of poetry itself." In England, Thomas Hardy remarked that there were two great things in the United States: the new American architecture and the poetry of Edna St. Vincent Millay.

By the late 20's and during the 30's, however, a change was noticeable. Critics were no longer unanimous in their praise of each new volume as it appeared. She was labeled too traditional, too romantic, too facile, too preoccupied

216

with herself and with love, immature, and unintellectual. This chorus of dissent first raised its voice after the publication of *The Buck in the Snow* at the end of 1928. In his review Max Eastman said, "It is supposed to be fashionable to find Edna Millay's new volume a trifle disappointing." Edna wrote to him saying that though the British reception of the book had been wonderful, he had been one of the very few New York critics who had a good word for it.

What had caused this change? Until 1928, when the first signs of it appeared, Edna had been a literary idol, the feminine poet laureate of the 1920's, and already something of a legend both as a poet and a symbol of the "new woman" of the twentieth century. The early poems were a novel combination of lighthearted wit and gently shadowed seriousness, reminiscent of the English Cavalier poets of the seventeenth century, with their crisp and clever cynicism not quite masking the wounded hearts beneath. They had made an instant appeal to the generation of the 1920's with its disillusion, romantic cynicism, and insistence upon individual freedom. She revealed their own sentiments to them, and they took her to their hearts.

But the public is hard on its heroes. The author of *The Buck in the Snow* was no longer quite the same as the author of *A Few Figs from Thistles*. As a woman, she was more mature, more experienced and reflective. As a poet, her technique and confidence had ripened. Her form had greater variety, and her statements, growing more charged with meaning, demanded closer attention from the reader.

Many of her early admirers had loved her for the impudent boldness, honesty, and timeliness of her themes. They had enjoyed quoting her relatively simple and easily remembered meters. This group of readers might lose interest in the more complex artist that was emerging; but what of the others, the more sophisticated readers and critics, who should certainly have been able to keep pace with her development and who should, if anything, have thought more highly than ever of her work?

These were drifting away from her because of a sharp new turn which poetry was taking at this time, a turn which was to lead it off in another direction from that taken by Edna Millay. In 1922, the very year for which she was awarded the Pulitzer Prize, T. S. Eliot's poem, "The Waste Land," was printed in *The Dial*. If any single event can be said to mark the end of the "poetic renaissance" which had begun in 1912, it was the appearance of this poem. By the same token, a new poetic era was inaugurated.

This was not immediately apparent. In 1922 and for several years thereafter, "The Waste Land" was the center of a violent controversy, with most readers frankly baffled by it. Many critics were irritated by its deliberate obscurity, classifying it with that other piece of "experimental gibberish," James Joyce's *Ulysses*, which came out in the same year. Others were repelled by the arid nihilism and cold despair which the poem seemed to emanate. Many simply dismissed it as unintelligible and ridiculous.

His meaning and methods may have been incomprehensible to others, but T. S. Eliot knew exactly what he was doing and went on doing it. He not only wrote poetry, he wrote essays about the art of writing poetry. He minutely scrutinized and discussed the work of a wide range of poets, from Dante to the present, and laid down a code of principles and standards for contemporary poets to follow. And in greater and greater numbers they did follow, until by the end of the decade his was the most influential voice speaking in the field of poetry. The ridicule ebbed away, to be replaced by an awed admiration. Not only poets but critics and readers of poetry began to apply his standards of judgment, often with little real thought or analysis on their own part, to everything they read. His ideas became the foundation of the "new criticism"; and it was against the rigidly applied formula growing out of these ideas that the work of Edna Millay came to be measured.

Edna poured her emotion and feeling into her poetry, and her personality illuminated everything she wrote; T. S. Eliot laid down the dictate that poetry must be "not a turning loose of emotion, but an escape from emotion . . . not the expression of personality, but an escape from personality." The poet, he decreed, must remain completely anonymous and put no part of his private self into his work.

Edna believed in communicating directly with her

readers. She wrote, she once said in an interview, about things that everyone can experience—love, death, nature. "My images," she said, "are homely, right out of the earth." She wanted people of every kind to understand her poetry, to read and memorize it and make it part of their lives. In "The Poet and His Book" she asks to be read by farmers, shepherds, sailors, scholars, hunters, men "that long for sleep," and those "that wake and revel." She asks boys and girls to "Mix me with your talk," and women to read her at their toil and at their pleasure and to "Mix me with your grief!" People were able to memorize her poems, she said, because so much of it was written in old-fashioned forms, "in the musical tradition . . . always known and loved."

Both the directness of her communication and her steady use of traditional forms ran counter to the new poetic fashions then emerging. The new poets and critics felt that poetry should not be explicit, it should not come right out and say what it meant; this was the function of prose. The "meaning" of a poem should be implicit, suggested by a series of images or symbols. Instead of naming or describing an emotion or an idea, the poet should use an image or symbol to produce the same emotion in the reader.

Direct statement was dropped entirely, leaving only indirect methods of communication. Many poets began to use remote mythological or literary allusions that the average reader could not possibly be familiar with, or symbols that had private meanings known only to the authors. As a result, many poems made no sense at all to the readers who had no way of knowing what the symbols or literary or mythological references stood for. Sometimes the meaning emerged only after long and close analysis, or required a process of unraveling more appropriate to a puzzle than a poem.

Poets became obscure and difficult to read. They grew critical of anyone who, like Edna Millay, remained clear and intelligible. They accused her of remaining on the surface of life instead of probing to the true nature of reality. Reality, they said, was constantly changing, and it was the poet's job to be aware of the new reality of each new moment, whereas Edna's poetry dealt with what she considered the continuing realities of love, death, nature, justice, and similar constants.

Because the world was always changing, poetic forms must keep changing, too, said the new writers; therefore, a poet must constantly experiment with new forms to meet the new conditions of the world. Modern life was increasingly complex, obscure, and difficult; therefore, poetry must be complex, obscure, and difficult. The old forms in poetry, they proclaimed, must be broken up, and new ones created, just as they had been in modern painting, music, and architecture.

Some of the new experimental poets evolved new and fluid forms which were quite exciting, and a new conception of freedom and flexibility was added to the art of poetry. But the revolt was often carried to an extreme. Traditional forms were rejected simply because they had been used before. The insistence upon originality and innovation for their own sakes often produced, in the end, work which was empty and synthetic and just as lifeless as the innovators had accused conventional verse of being.

In the midst of all the experimentation, some of it pretty wild, Edna Millay went right on using established verse forms—the sonnet, the ballad, the lyric. Though her own use of these forms became more flexible, she never abandoned them, finding them entirely suited to her needs. To abandon them just for the sake of an artificial and meaningless "originality" would have seemed to her absurd.

There was still another divergence between her and the new schools of poetry and criticism. Many of the new poets, particularly Eliot, saw the contemporary world as devoid of meaning. They projected the image of modern man as either small, mean, and empty-souled, or else lost and confused, living in an ugly and commercialized universe. "Our own period," said Eliot, "is one of decline." "The Waste Land," with its rootless cosmopolitans going through the dreary routine of their sterile lives, became the symbol of the spiritual malady that, in the eyes of many of these poets, afflicted the modern world.

Eliot himself was not filled with despair. He believed that salvation was possible by restoring the broken ties between man and some force outside himself—a force to be found in religion, tradition, myth, the life-death cycle of nature—anything that would restore man's faith in the universe. Eliot found his own personal redemption in a return to religion; other poets embraced a world of imagination or myth which went beyond the limitations of the material world and gave it meaning. If you could accept Eliot's prescription, you were saved. Otherwise you remained one of his "hollow men," living in an unreal and soulless wasteland. It was a cheerless prospect for those who refused to accept his insistence on a faith in something outside of man himself.

Edna Millay had no sympathy with Eliot's point of view; she felt that he was a "death-bringer." When discussing Eliot with friends, she remarked that he was a profound scholar, but involved and wordy and singularly unpoetic. In 1949 she wrote a satire in verse against him in which she says, according to her description in a letter, nothing abusive about him—she is "merely murderous." Unfortunately, this series of about twenty poems was never published. She dismissed Ezra Pound, who so strongly influenced Eliot, with the comment: "Ezra's such a short-weight pound."

Her passionate faith in the creations of this world was diametrically opposed to the bleak views held by many of the new poets. Man and the manifestations of nature held meaning enough for her—she did not require bolstering from religion or symbolic myth. Her answer to the new poets and critics can be seen in several sonnets in her last book, *Mine the Harvest*. One of these begins:

Not, to me, less lavish—though my dreams have been
  splendid—
Than dreams, have been the hours of the actual day:

Immediate reality is marvelous enough for her:

Music, and painting, poetry, love, and grief,
Had they been more intense, I could not have borne,—
Yet, not, I think, through stout endurance lacked;
Rather, because the budding and the falling leaf
Were one, and wonderful,—not to be torn
Apart: I ask of dream: seem like the fact.

She knew well enough how many things were wrong
with the world. She herself, in poems like "Epitaph for
the Race of Man" and even more in the poetry of her
next period, attacked the evils and weaknesses and confusions of mankind. Nevertheless, she never loathes or
degrades man. She is proud of that "doomed and splendid
race." In the second "Read history" sonnet, she says:

For trouble comes to all of us: the rat
Has courage, in adversity, to fight;
But what a shining animal is man,
Who knows, when pain subsides, that is not that,
For worse than that must follow—yet can write
Music; can laugh; play tennis; even plan.

She believed that men were capable of making a better
world, not quickly or by simple political means, but by
gradually developing the potential for good that lay
within them.

In another sonnet, "It is the fashion now to wave aside," she sums up the contemporary revolt against traditional themes and techniques in poetry:

Straightforwardness is wrong, evasion right;
It is correct, de rigueur, to deride.
What fumy wits these modern wags expose,
For all their versatility: Voltaire,
Who wore to bed a night-cap, and would close,
In fear of drafts, all windows, could declare
In antique stuffiness, a phrase that blows
Still through men's smoky minds, and clears the air.

There are fashions in poetry as in everything else. By the end of the 1920's to admire Eliot and the new poetry and to downgrade all poets not of his school, had become "the thing to do."

Edna Millay was too firmly entrenched and her work too inherently effective despite its divergence from the rising tide of new poetry, to go into eclipse, no matter what the fashion. Her particular vein of feeling and her superb lyrical skill would always find responsive listeners. She would continue to be admired and appreciated, and her books would continue to be widely read. Over three-quarters of a million copies of her books would be sold during her lifetime. Nevertheless, her honeymoon with the critics was over. Dissenting voices would appear in the general chorus of approval, and many readers would, for a time at least, be diverted to the new heralds of the poetic world.

She remained impartial in her own judgments. Fashions in poetry did not affect her in the slightest, either as a writer or as a lover of poetry. Actually, she admired some of the new poets and their idols among the earlier writers. Robinson Jeffers, a new poet of the 20's, and Donne and Gerard Manley Hopkins who served as inspirations for the new poets, were favorites of her own. When she was in California, she went to see Jeffers in his tower at Carmel. She memorized at least a third of Hopkins' poetry, an especially difficult feat but one which she found "great fun, very exciting." And when that arch experimentalist, E. E. Cummings, applied for a Guggenheim Fellowship, she wrote a detailed three-thousand word analysis of his verse and recommended that he be granted the award.

Nothing could shake her independence. She examined the ideas and work of others carefully and with scrupulous fairness, but her own ideas and the shape of her work would remain entirely hers, no matter how unfashionable, or difficult, or even painful it might prove.

23.

Poetry and Propaganda

Dear Islander, I envy you:
I'm very fond of islands, too;
And few the pleasures I have known
Which equalled being left alone.
Yet matters from without intrude
At times upon my solitude:
A forest fire, a dog run mad,
A neighbour stripped of all he had
By swindlers, or the shrieking plea
For help, of stabbed Democracy.
                —From "There Are No Islands Any More."

IN 1940 Edna wrote, "My life has always gone abruptly
and breath-takingly up and down, like a roller-coaster!"
At the end of the 1930's it started on one of the down-
slopes. Her health, her fortune, and her poetry were all
involved. Above everything there loomed World War
II, to whose tensions and disasters Edna was intensely
vulnerable.

Her health, never robust since her twenties, had received a severe setback from the accident in the summer
of 1936 when she was thrown from the Steepletop station
wagon. The injury to her right arm and back turned out
to be more serious than originally suspected. For a few

227

years she had attributed the pain in her arm to strain as a result of playing too much tennis, or practicing the piano too long, or overzealously pulling weeds from the Steepletop lawns. She thought she was troubled by bursitis, never connecting the pain with the accident. By 1939, however, the pain had become continuous, and deeper investigation showed that several nerves in her spine had been injured.

There now began the dreary, discouraging round of seeking relief. Everything was tried: nerve surgery, massage, X-ray, infra-red-ray, several long regimens of medication. She was in the hospital three times in one year alone. For five months she slept on a plank. Thousands of dollars were spent on medical and hospital bills. Nothing helped very much. At times the pain was so excruciating that she could hardly work—using a typewriter, even handling a knife and fork at meals, increased the pain unbearably.

Throughout it all, Eugen nursed her with greater devotion than ever. He took care of all her needs, even learning how to inject the morphine which had been prescribed to give her some measure of relief, though he always hated to do it. He was consumed with worry over her condition.

Her illness intensified the impulse to withdraw from the world. Neither she nor Eugen answered any but the most urgent letters, and even these were often put aside for months or years. For long periods they saw practically no one.

During 1941 she began to improve. She was able to say in March that for one whole day she felt almost entirely free from pain. Toward the end of the year she wrote to Witter Bynner that she believed she was really cured.

It was like the releasing of a great clamp that had tightened around her life. Before the release was complete, however, a new and formidable pressure was applied. Eugen's income had come largely from investments in Java. Because of the war, these were all lost, and the Boissevains were plunged into the deepest financial difficulties. Edna's books were earning royalties, but the breakoff of the major part of their income left them far behind in meeting their expenses, particularly since her heavy medical bills continued for a time after Eugen lost his money. Steepletop had to be mortgaged and she was forced to ask her publisher for one advance after another. With Eugen's fortune gone, she wrote to her editor, it was now up to her to earn what they needed.

It was an ironical return to the difficulties of her childhood. In a letter to Ferdinand Earle, the judge of *The Lyric Year* contest who had wanted to give her the five hundred dollar prize, she said it had seemed a fortune then, and added ruefully that it seemed almost a fortune to her now, too.

Above all these personal tribulations was World War II. Everything that happened—every step that led to the final conflagration—seemed to bear out Edna Millay's worst forebodings, her gloomiest predictions, about the self-destructive tendencies of the human race. The Sacco-Vanzetti affair had awakened her to a keener understanding of how these destructive forces might operate. In *Wine from These Grapes*, published in 1934, her disappointment in mankind is reflected in several poems, particularly in the two Sacco-Vanzetti sonnets and in "My Spirit, Sore from Marching," "Apostrophe to Man," and "Epitaph for the Race of Man."

Two years later, in 1936, a significant move toward war was taken when Hitler sent troops into the Rhineland in violation of the Versailles Treaty. From then on, one crisis followed another. Hitler annexed Austria and Czechoslovakia and in September, 1939, touched off World War II with his invasion of Poland. Edna's anguished dismay over these events was expressed in *Huntsman, What Quarry?* (1939), in poems like "Say that We Saw Spain Die," "Underground System," and "Czecho-Slovakia."

Her attitude toward war began to change. Earlier, in "Apostrophe to Man," she had lashed out at the "detestable race," had mocked *"homo* called *sapiens"* for preparing to go to war again. Now she began to realize that there are times when it is necessary to arm and even fight against evil. In the second of the "Three Sonnets in Tetrameter" she says that even the rose must put on the armor of the thorn.

When the Germans overran Holland in 1940, the war struck the Boissevains personally. Most of Eugen's family were still there. All communication was broken off and for the next few years Edna and Eugen were filled with devastating anxiety.

Nearly everyone in America was opposed to Hitler and to fascism; nearly everyone felt he must be stopped and democracy restored to Europe. However, on the question of just what or how much the United States should do about the situation, opinion was sharply divided. Most Americans did not want to go to war. Many felt that though Hitler's actions were reprehensible, they concerned only Europe. The war was strictly a foreign affair and we should stay out of it. Others, worn out by the ravages of the depression, or with young sons of fighting age, were reluctant to face the catastrophe of war however just the cause might be. Above all, there was the belief that America itself was in no danger. Even a victorious Hitler could not cross the Atlantic to invade our shores.

A sizeable minority of Americans, however, felt the danger was very real, and that as soon as Hitler finished mopping up Europe, he would turn his aggressions upon America, aided from the east by Japan. One portion of this minority was in favor of helping Britain with money and supplies—all aid short of war. A still smaller group was in favor of all-out assistance, even if it led to entering the war ourselves. It was not a matter of sympathy with the defeated nations, argued this group; we must fight out of sheer self-preservation. Otherwise we would become the last of the sitting democratic ducks to be eliminated by Hitler on his march to world supremacy.

Among this last group was Edna Millay. It was a great

wrench for her to abandon her pacifist views, but she felt that awful though war was, it was preferable to the slavery that nonresistance to Fascist aggression would bring. *Aria da Capo* had been a protest against war as cruel and useless. But this war was being thrust upon us, and to ignore the onrushing enemy, to refuse to fight him in self-defense, would be unrealistic. We had no choice any more, she felt, we must be prepared to fight in order to remain alive and free.

She was distressed at the blindness of her countrymen to their own peril and the slowness of their leaders to act. She decided that at whatever cost to herself, she must rouse the United States to the imminent dangers which threatened it. She began writing poems which she frankly admitted were pure propaganda. They were written at great speed, with no pause for the slow, careful polishing which she had always before given to her work. She was convinced there was no time to lose.

One of the first, written in the desperate days just before the fall of France, was headed *"There Are No Islands Any More,* May 1940, (Lines Written in Passion and in Deep Concern for England, France, and My Own Country)." Its theme was taken from Hitler's assertion that militarily speaking there were no longer any islands—although she might also have had in mind John Donne's "No man is an *Iland,* intire of it selfe; every man is a peece of the Continent, a part of the *maine.*" Hitler, of course, was speaking of the fact that Britain's insular position which had protected her from invasion for so many centuries was no longer impregnable against the devices of modern warfare. Edna extends the idea to encompass America. We, too, are no longer safe—no separate enclave of Democracy can close its eyes and pretend the enemy cannot reach its sea-surrounded haven:

> (*The tidal wave devours the shore:*
> *There* are *no islands any more*)

She begins with a sharp attack on the isolationist position and ends with a plea to help Britain and France in their fight against what is our enemy as well as theirs:

> *Lest French and British fighters, deep*
> *In battle, needing guns and sleep,*
> *For lack of aid be overthrown,*
> *And we be left to fight alone.*

After its initial appearance in newspapers and periodicals, the poem was printed as a separate leaflet. Though the Boissevains were already hard pressed for money, Edna announced that the proceeds of its sale would be donated to the British War Relief. The following spring, a canteen ambulance was bought with the money earned by the poem and presented by Edna to the chairman of the British-American Ambulance Corps. It was shipped to the British forces in Africa.

Later in 1940 the poem was included in a new volume of Edna's poetry, *Make Bright the Arrows*, subtitled "1940 Notebook." It is a collection, says the bookjacket, "on which the ink is scarcely dry." She herself called it "a book of impassioned propaganda" rather than a book of verse. It consists chiefly of poems which are arguments for preparedness and for aid to France and Britain. In his first address to Congress, George Washington had said, "To be prepared for war is one of the most effectual means of preserving peace." This is the main theme of *Make Bright the Arrows*. It is a passionate attempt to shake Americans loose from their isolationism or indifference. She uses irony, scorn, pathos, sympathy, warnings, and threats. She severely criticizes the complacent Americans who refuse to take heed of obvious danger signals. She accuses them of being soft, lazy, greedy, and selfish. Even when they recognize danger, they do not want the bother of doing anything about it.

She sent an inscribed copy of the book to Charlotte Babcock Sills, her Vassar roommate. To Edna's dismay, Charlotte, the mother of three sons of draft age, was distressed by what she considered an effort to rush her boys to war. Edna explained her point of view in a long letter. She was trying, she wrote, ". . . not to get this country into war, but to keep it out of war." She was urging it to arm, not for the purpose of engaging aggressively in war, but as the best defense against it:

> *Stock well the quiver*
> *With arrows bright:*
> *The bowman feared*
> *Need never fight.*

Make bright the arrows,
O peaceful and wise!
Gather the shields
Against surprise.

The best way to prevent Germany and Japan from attacking us, she felt, was to build up our defenses and show our readiness to fight if necessary. We must also help Britain in her fight against our enemy, otherwise we, too, will be crushed.

Though she had no sons, like Charlotte, to give to the war, she was offering the one thing she did have to give: her reputation as a poet. "How many more books of propaganda poetry containing as much bad verse as this one does, that reputation can withstand . . . without becoming irretrievably lost, I do not know. . . . Have you the slightest conception of what this reputation means to me, who have been building it carefully for more than twenty years . . . ?" Because of her "furious haste," the poems were "faulty and unpolished." Thousands of her readers, she said, would never forgive her for writing this book. "Thus, you see, the dearest thing in life I possess which might possibly be of help to my country, has already gone over the top, in the hope that your sons need never go to war."

The attack on Pearl Harbor which finally brought America into the war was bitter proof that Edna's fears had been justified. Being proved right brought her no consolation. She had been grieved by some of the adverse criticism of *Make Bright the Arrows*, but she was infinitely more distressed that "in spite of all that so many of us tried so hard to do," Pearl Harbor had been allowed to happen.

Once America was in the war, Edna redoubled her efforts. She wrote war poems, worked for the Writers' War Board and the Red Cross, took part in symposiums and conferences—all, of course, without pay and despite her preference for seclusion. In some instances, she even had to pay her own expenses. This was at a time when she and Eugen needed money desperately and her energies were depleted by anxiety and ill health. In the middle of 1941 she had made an album of four records of her poetry for R.C.A. Victor Records. A volume of *Collected Sonnets* was also brought out, followed later by a companion volume, *Collected Lyrics*. The proceeds from the sales of these books and records helped, but the Boissevains' need continued.

Nevertheless, in spite of her own personal difficulties, she continued to do whatever she could to help the war program. She and Eugen took war measures, such as rationing, so seriously that even though they were entitled to extra gasoline because Steepletop was a working farm, they used a horse and buggy instead of an automobile for local trips, and shut off their gasoline-consuming electric generator, using candlelight instead.

On June 10, 1942, the German government proclaimed its destruction of the tiny village of Lidice in Czechoslovakia. The village had been suspected of harboring the killers of Reinhard Heydrich, the Nazi administrator of the region, a man so brutal that he had been nick-named "the Hangman." Though the suspicions were never proved, the Nazis decided to make an object lesson of Lidice and set about it with a methodical efficiency that horrified the world. All the men, including the priest, were herded into the village square and shot. The women were taken off to concentration camps and the children put into German institutions. The Nazis then set fire to the houses and the church, completing the destruction with shell-fire until the town had been razed to the ground.

When news of the outrage reached the United States, the Writers' War Board decided to commemorate Lidice and asked Edna Millay to write a poem about it. She produced a long dramatic narrative in verse describing the life and death of the village and ending with a plea to America to grasp the full menace of Nazi ruthlessness. She wanted to prod her countrymen into a more immediate sense of danger and into a more energetic effort against an enemy whose power she felt they were still underrating.

The Murder of Lidice was broadcast over NBC on October 19, with Alexander Woollcott, Paul Muni, and Clifton Fadiman taking part. It was also short-waved to England and other countries and, at the same time, Spanish and Portuguese translations were beamed to South America. At the end of the performance Edna was brought to the platform, and the bound manuscript of the broadcast was auctioned off for a thousand dollars for the benefit of Czechoslovakian war relief. The original version of the poem was published in pamphlet form by Harper.

Edna was receiving steady public recognition. In 1940 she had been elected to the American Academy of Arts and Letters. At its annual dinner on January 31, 1943, the Poetry Society of America awarded her its Gold Medal for "meritorious work and abiding interest in the humanities." In April she was selected as one of twelve distinguished American women to participate in a symposium sponsored by *The New York Times* on rebuilding the postwar world.

Her personal troubles, however, continued. In July she wrote to Harper asking for help again, saying, "I'm stone broke." In addition to their financial worries, the Boissevains were still deeply concerned over the fate of Eugen's cousins in Holland. They heard later that one of them had been tortured and killed by the Nazi invaders; others had narrow escapes, and all of them suffered under the German occupation. At the very beginning of the war, one of Edna's cousins, Lieut. Col. George Ricker of the U.S. Army General Staff, had been reported missing with his plane. The final blow came in September when Kathleen, who had left her job in a war plant to apply for admission to the WACs, suddenly collapsed and died.

As though to offset these personal tragedies, the war took an upward turn. In May, 1943, the Nazis were driven out of North Africa. By the end of the year Allied forces had landed in southern Italy. On June 6, 1944, "D-Day," the second front was opened. Two million British and American troops were thrown against the German fortifications in Normandy.

Behind the invasion front, an anxious world held its breath and waited for whatever driblets of news the military authorities could release. In New York the National Broadcasting Company ran a twenty-four-hour program of news, analyses, prayers, and special items appropriate to the day. Among these was the "Poem and Prayer for an Invading Army," written by Edna St. Vincent Millay and read by Ronald Colman.

She invokes protection and care for the soldiers of the invading forces, but the climax of the poem returns to one of her persistent fears: the potentiality for destructiveness and evil in the hearts of men. She concludes with the plea that when our soldiers return we must see that they do not find in their own country "the very monster which they sallied forth to conquer and to quell." The monster, the "hideous beast," is this human capacity for evil which the Nazis embodied, and against which the war had to be fought. Its manifestations are hatred, greed, and bigotry, all of which she urges her listeners to erase from their own hearts.

This inner depravity of man had always disturbed her profoundly. When it reached its peak in the years before and during World War II, it roused her, as one reviewer put it, to a "noble fury," a "quick and passionate loathing," which had driven her into writing hastily and intemperately. In many instances she allowed her emotions to run away with her war poems. In some of the pieces the emotion comes through strongly and movingly. Often, however, the verses consist of bluntly argumentative, polemical ideas, and the reader remains outside them, untouched. She scolds her readers instead of moving them.

She was severely criticized for her propaganda verse by reviewers who insisted upon judging them as poetry instead of as propaganda. Some of the reviews of *Make Bright the Arrows* had been, in her own words, "insolent to the point of being really 'actionable.'" One reviewer said that she lashed out at the warring world "like a lady octopus caught in a whirlpool," and that the book contained nothing more than "fancy doggerel."

But Edna had never intended the book to be taken as serious poetry. She had planned it as a paperbound leaflet, to be thrown away after it had served its purpose. Her publishers, however, had gone ahead and issued it in the same hard-cover format as her other books and, to her deep distress, the critics had taken it seriously, as though she herself considered it in the same light as the rest of her work. They ignored the implication of her subtitle, "1940 Notebook." Her own conception of the nature of the book was revealed in the inscription she wrote in Floyd Dell's copy: "Dear Floyd, don't be a critic of poetry while you read this book—just be a recorder of human

Where right through wrong might make its way, and be;
If from all taint of indignation, free
Must be my art, and thereby fugitive
From all that threatens it—why—let me give
To moles my dubious immortality.

Nevertheless, despite these justifications, she suffered greatly not only from the harsh criticism her work received but from her own consciousness of what she felt were the "acres of bad poetry" she had written. ". . . I can tell you from my own experience," she wrote to Edmund Wilson, "that there is nothing on this earth which can so much get on the nerves of a good poet, as the writing of bad poetry."

It all became too much for her. In the summer of 1944, after five years of writing nothing but propaganda verse, and with her emotions already strained by illness and money troubles, she had a nervous breakdown. For a long time, she had to remain in Doctors Hospital in New York. She had given herself generously and selflessly, and was as much a victim of the war as if she had been a soldier fighting on the military front.

reactions. (Except in the case of the *good* poen
are a few)."

In using her verse as an instrument of propag
taking part in social and political movements, she
course, in good company. Dante, Milton, Shelley.
Dickens had all used their pens in similar caus
many of Edna's contemporaries insisted that it
the poet's function to take part in such movemen
use their poetic talents for the writing of prop
They felt that a poet's first, and indeed only, duty
his craft, even during a great national emergency
wanted to help in the war effort, let him do so as a
not as a poet. Let him drive an ambulance, work
Red Cross, buy war bonds.

Edna Millay, however, felt that it was precise
poet, writing verse to rouse people to action, th
could best help the war effort. If her poetry and
reputation suffered as a result, it was worth the sac
"This is no time to think of one's reputation whe
world is in the midst of disaster," she said in an inter
". . . today it is the duty of the adult poet to wor
the perpetuation of a world in which poetry still c
written. . . ."

She defended her position in several of her later
nets. One of the best of these begins:

And if I die, because that part of me
Which part alone of me had chance to live,
Chose to be honour's threshing-floor, a sieve

24.

Last Years

Happiness, happiness, which once I held in my hand,
Does it persist?
Does it exist,
Perhaps, in some foreign land?

—Collected Poems.

IN 1945, with the war over, the Boissevains resumed the regular course of their lives at Steepletop and Ragged Island. Edna had recovered from her breakdown of the previous summer, but she was still under a strain. Vincent Sheean, who saw her in the summer of 1945, describes her as "very frightened, small, and withdrawn. . . . Her temperament was so variable that it was impossible to tell what mood might overwhelm her next; and she was obviously so painfully sensitive that any untoward phrase or sudden noise could thrust her into a private hell from which she might not emerge for days."

She was suffering from the worst affliction that can beset a writer: she could not write. Of all the occupational hazards in art, the most painful is the inability to work, a blight that can descend at any moment and without warning. For Edna, who might be said to have lived for the creation of poetry, this period of aridity must have been agonizing.

243

Another source of depression during this year was the long, incurable illness of Arthur Ficke, and his death at the end of November. The Fickes, living all these years at Hardhack in nearby Hillsdale, had been fairly close neighbors of the Boissevains. Edna had never gotten over her feeling for Arthur. In one of her last letters to him she wrote about "how terribly, how sickeningly, in love with you I had been." She admitted that she had written the sonnet, "And you as well must die, belovèd dust," to him. At his funeral she read this sonnet, together with passages from Milton's "Lycidas," which had been one of Arthur's favorite poems.

Eugen watched over Edna more protectively than ever, guarding his "frail treasure," wrote Max Eastman, "like a dedicated dragon." When, on occasion, they saw a few selected friends, he eased over any difficult moments with his jovial warmth. When she could not bear the strain of the external world, he ruthlessly excluded it. "One felt on entering Steepletop," said Eastman, "that some very fragile piece of china, inestimable in value, was in unstable equilibrium upstairs. . . ."

During the months of illness and recovery, she continued her lifelong habit of committing poems to memory. In letters written at this time, she mentions learning by heart a lyric of Catullus, Matthew Arnold's "The Scholar Gypsy," Keats' "The Eve of St. Agnes" and "Lamia," and Shelley's "To the West Wind" and "Hymn to Intellectual Beauty." ". . . I have them all now," she wrote to Edmund Wilson. "And what evil thing can ever again brush me with its wings?"

Gradually she recovered her spirits and her ability to write. In the summer of 1946 she was able to send Wilson three new poems—"Ragged Island," "Tranquility at length, when autumn comes," and "To a Snake." By 1947 she could think of a new volume of poetry. In a letter to her publisher, Harper & Brothers, she said she was writing again and that the new poems were good. If Harper would be patient, there would be another book.

She refused to be hurried or pressured in any way. She explained that because of the "sloppy, garrulous and un-integrated" propaganda verse she had written during the war, she was now more careful and self-critical, and was therefore writing more slowly, than ever before. Her concern with high standards and with her reputation had, if anything, increased. Harper suggested several publish-ing ventures at this time which would have added to her income with little effort on her part. Though she could certainly have used the money, she rejected the schemes as unworthy.

One of Harper's propositions was to publish a volume of her collected dramatic works. Edna regretfully vetoed this because she felt that of her seven dramatic works only *Aria da Capo* was of any real significance. In a letter, she goes into a detached, critical analysis of each of the others, concluding that a book containing all of them would be a mistake.

Another suggestion was that Harper bring out a book of *The Love Poems of Edna St. Vincent Millay*, with a foreword explaining the circumstances under which the poems were written. Presumably, this would include a statement telling about whom the verses were. It would be, in effect, a romantic autobiography.

She vigorously rejected the idea. Such a foreword, she explained in an incisive letter to Harper, would be a violation of her long-established reticence. Throughout her literary career she had consistently refused to make in print any statement about any poem she had ever published. Even though she agreed with Harper that such a book would attract new readers, she declared that the very quality which drew such readers would lose her the esteem of the more sensitive "and by me the most valued" of the readers she already had.

In another letter she warned Harper that no one must ever presume to change a word of her poems. Nothing of hers, she insisted, must be altered after her death. "Only I, who know what I mean to say, and how I want to say it, am competent to deal with such matters," she wrote, ". . . . the faults as well as the virtues of this poetry, are my own. . . ."

Throughout her correspondence, even in the letters written when she was ill and distraught, there runs this strong conviction of the rightness of her own ideas. Perhaps it was part of the New England toughness which had persisted, no matter how the circumstances of her life may have changed. There often seemed in Edna Millay an echo of the old New England conscience, the heritage of the Puritan colonists, which amounted to an almost rigid inflexibility of principle, and which Edna might have absorbed from her early life in Maine. Perhaps it was that which had driven her during the war to yield her poetic reputation in the service of her country, a contribution which other poets had considered unnecessary and for which she had been attacked. Max Eastman once remarked that working in a munitions factory or knitting socks for soldiers might have been a better gift to the war effort than producing bad poetry but would not have involved the quality of sacrifice demanded by the rigid moralism of New England. He called it a "stern revel in self-mortification."

The extreme adherence to principle also appeared in the affair of the Academy of American Poets. This was a newly-formed organization which planned to give fellowships of five thousand dollars each to selected poets, to enable them to devote a year exclusively to writing poetry without having to worry about money. Edna was asked to serve on the Board of Chancellors. She carefully studied all the legal documents of the organization and then declined. A chancellor, she explained, is supposed to determine whether a poet was worthy of the fellowship, but she had discovered that the fellowship was not worthy of the poet. It put too many "onerous and humiliating" obligations upon him, she charged, in the form of reports on his work and restrictions on his nonpoetic occupations.

Within the next few months the terms of the award were changed and the offending restrictions removed, in accordance with her criticisms. Less than two years later, at the end of 1949, Edna Millay herself was awarded one of the fellowships. It came at one of the lowest points in her life, when she badly needed the money and the publicity and encouragement such an event would bring.

On the night of the formal banquet of the Academy, when the awards were to be announced, Edna had still not notified the president of her acceptance. Chancellor Max Eastman decided to telephone her at Steepletop. It took almost an hour to reach her. Her receiver was off the hook, as it often was in those days, because she did not want to be disturbed by telephone calls. A neighbor had to be found to drive over and ask her to hang up the receiver so that the call could be put through. When Eastman was finally able to talk with her, she said she would accept nothing from the Academy of American Poets. He argued with her, explaining that the Academy had changed its by-laws as she herself had suggested. He reminded her how much she needed the five thousand dollars. But all she would say was:

"It is true, Max, I do need the money desperately, but I can't take it. I could not be happy if I betrayed my ideals in this thing. There's no use arguing."

And there was no use, though Eastman tried. She remained absolutely firm in her refusal even though, under the new terms of the fellowship, it was hard to see what ideals would have been betrayed by her acceptance.

In the late 1940's she was able to work more or less steadily again, putting together the poems that were to comprise her last book, *Mine the Harvest*. They were difficult years: though she was writing, there were still periods of great anxiety. There were financial problems. Harper came to her rescue by sending her regular monthly payments instead of the uncertain and varying amounts of the usual royalty earnings.

She and Eugen aged during these years. Her delicate little figure grew heavier, her eyes became heavy-lidded. The bright spirit of the 1920's had given way to the war-weary anguish of the 1940's.

All the bright young people—and the bright young ideas—of the 1920's had aged. The "free spirits" of the Village had settled down, raised families, come to terms with the encroaching responsibilities of maturity. Their bold new ideas of emancipation and experimentation had long been accepted and taken for granted, replaced by new perplexities of a new era. In a number of instances unrestricted freedom had proved as unsatisfactory as un-deviating conformity. It had been the fate of some of Edna's contemporaries to achieve the first and then suffer the disappointment of not finding it a permanent solu-tion after all. Most of them were now living more or less quietly, accepting more or less graciously the fact that they were no longer the shining lights, the new hopes, of the world. Many of the glamorous names had dimmed, hardly recognized by a new generation with leaders and idols of its own.

The Boissevains lived a more isolated existence than ever, seeing very few people, rarely leaving Steepletop except to go to Ragged Island. They did not even attend the Berkshire Music Festival at Tanglewood, scarcely an hour's drive away, though music had remained an integral part of Edna's life. She was fearful of strangers and disliked going out into the world. There were periods when they had no telephone—"we got sick and tired of its insistence and its inefficiency, so we up and yanked it out." Eugen had to hike down into Austerlitz whenever they felt it really necessary to call someone. Steepletop became more than ever a refuge, removed from interruptions and distractions.

An echo of her resistance to the intruding world can be found in two of the poems in *Mine the Harvest*. One of them is "Cave Canem," in which she complains that

Importuned through the mails, accosted over the tele-
phone, overtaken by running footsteps, caught by
the sleeve, the servant of strangers,
While amidst the haste and confusion lover and friend
quietly step into the unreachable past,
I throw bright time to chickens in an untidy yard.

Through timidity, dislike of anger and of "faces with no love in them," she avoids "the looming visitor." Though she wishes him well, she hates him because his presence might force her to pretend that he is welcome, that she is free to sit with him. Meanwhile, important work goes undone, "the potted roses wilt in the crate or the sonnet cools" while she listens respectfully to ideas which were already old and familiar in her childhood.

The other is a sonnet, "What chores these churls do

put upon the great," which describes how petty interruptions can destroy the creative flow of the artist's work, breaking in upon him

> . . . *till broken thought receded*
> *And ebbed in foam, like ocean down a beach.*

This has always been the dilemma of the artist: to have the strength to push the world away so that he can concentrate on his work, even when his withdrawal might seem unkind or self-centered. He must determine the exact degree to which he can safely cut himself off without losing contact with the world altogether. He must perform the delicate seesaw operation of being part of the human fabric and yet outside it, at properly balanced intervals.

Did Edna Millay successfully achieve this delicate balance? Had she thrown herself too completely into the context of active life when she devoted herself exclusively to propaganda verse before and during the war, and was she withdrawing too completely in these postwar years?

With Edna Millay, it was especially difficult to draw the line between the poet and the woman. Her life was in its own way as much a work of art as her poetry. It has been said of her that she created a dramatic atmosphere in which she constantly moved, and which surrounded others whenever they came within the orbit of her personality. The elusive, volatile nymph of the Village, the cosmopolitan sophisticate of the later years, the impas-

sioned defender of principle, the shy recluse of Steepletop, were all as fascinating and significant as the poetry
itself. Both as a woman and as a poet she stood for beauty,
love, and freedom. She had expressed these in her verse
with an almost extravagant courage and passion.

For her to parcel out her energies into carefully measured segments would have been impossible. It was not in
her to hold herself back. Nor was she ever deterred by the
sheer magnitude of any self-commitment. "Enormity,"
she had once written in connection with a difficult relationship, "does not frighten me; it is only among tremendous things that I feel happy and at ease. . . ." Modera-
tion was not one of her outstanding characteristics.

By the summer of 1949 she was in high gear again. In
June she wrote to Harper that she had been working "all
day and during a great portion of the night" for about
seven months.

But just as her energies had gathered renewed force, as
the flow of her work was at last running unimpeded,
everything was jolted to a shocking halt. In August
Eugen went to see a doctor. He did not feel sick, but he
had a persistent cough. An X-ray examination revealed a
serious condition in his lung. He went to the Deaconess
Hospital in Boston for an operation toward the end of
the month. The operation appeared successful and he
seemed to be recovering, but on August 30 he suddenly
died. He was sixty-nine years old.

Eugen had been more than a beloved husband to Edna.
He had also been guardian, nurse, companion, protector.

As the world had receded, as fewer people had taken part in her life, he had come to encompass within himself even more of the world for her. She, who had written so much about the impermanence of love, had in the end found twenty-six years of happiness with him.

She broke down completely after his death, and once again spent a long period of illness in Doctors Hospital. When she was able to return to Steepletop, she refused to have anyone with her. For the next year she lived entirely alone, insisting that was the only way she could go through with it and not break down again. During the winter she was even more isolated when she had the telephone wires taken down. The extreme cold had produced a humming sound in the wires which she could not stand, and which had kept her awake at night. When she did have phone service, she arranged it so that no incoming calls could be received, because "If it rang, I would hear his footsteps as he ran to answer it." When friends wanted to visit her, she put them off, spending even the holidays alone. She observed Christmas Eve by playing and singing carols to herself; on New Year's Eve, she telephoned to Eugen's family in Holland. She knew they would be worried about her, since they loved her "as if I were their own kin; as I do them."

Mary Herron, the postmistress of Austerlitz, helped her considerably by taking care of business details and answering letters, especially the large number expressing sympathy. John Pinnie, the farmer who had been at Steepletop almost from the beginning, came every day to do the chores. A neighbor came in at intervals to help with the housekeeping. Aside from these contacts, her solitude remained virtually unbroken.

During the twenty-six years of their marriage, Eugen had taken care of everything. Now when details like bills and taxes and all the minutiae of running a household were suddenly thrust upon her, she did not even know where to look for essential documents. Perhaps Eugen had overprotected her. There were people who felt that he had babied her, and had encouraged in her a streak of self-indulgent egotism. Perhaps a poet needs an immediate contact with reality, even in the form of dealing with the mundane details of everyday domesticity from which Eugen had shielded her. This might have given an added vigor and a more complete, or an earlier, maturity to her work.

Others felt that Eugen had not only contributed to the development of her talents by releasing her from distracting trivia but had exerted a direct influence upon the poetry itself. Deems Taylor, in his tribute to Edna Millay for the American Academy of Arts and Letters, says that Eugen had an "uncanny sense of English poetry, and was as merciless a critic of her work as she was herself."

With Eugen gone, and with the first shattering effects of his loss behind her, Edna's old qualities of independence and courage reasserted themselves. For years, before Eugen entered her life, she had managed to take care of herself and at the same time become one of the foremost lyrists of the country; she would take care of herself again and produce still another book.

She survived the agony—this was her own word—of the first winter without Eugen. Now she was faced with a greater ordeal, the spring. "You wonder how I am going to stand the spring," she wrote to Mary Herron; "I'm wondering myself. . . . And I'm plenty scared. Not scared that I shan't muddle through in some way or other. Just scared. Shrinking from being hurt too much. Scared the way I used to be as a child, when I had to go to the dentist."

When she saw the first dandelion of spring, remembering how excited Eugen used to get at the sight, she stared at it "with a kind of horror." And then, "my face just crumpled up and cried."

Somehow she got through the spring into summer. She could not face going to Ragged Island but refused to sell it, planning to go back eventually when she felt able to bear it. *The Saturday Evening Post* commissioned her to write a Thanksgiving poem, which helped her get through part of the summer. She applied herself with great seriousness, asking the library at Lenox to send her whatever books they might have about the Pilgrim Fathers, and then, when the poem was almost finished, scrapped it as being unsuitable and wrote an entirely new one. She said she knew she was "making a big fuss about a small piece of work,—but it is so wonderful to be writing again!" Writing, she said, was her only hope.

Her letters at the end of this summer suggest an easing of the strain. She was ready to see people. She was working on new poems. She had also put her house in order.

When Edmund Wilson had visited Steepletop in 1948, the living room had seemed to him run-down and shabby. By the fall of 1950 the furniture had been freshly recovered and polished, the floors waxed. She was even able to look out at the autumn glowing from the hills around Steepletop and write:

> I will control myself, or go inside.
> I will not flaw perfection with my grief.
> Handsome, this day: no matter who has died.

This was found in her last notebook and was perhaps one of the last fragments of verse she wrote.

On the night of October 18, 1950, alone as usual, she was reading the proofs of a translation of the *Aeneid* by Rolfe Humphries. She read all night long, until dawn of the 19th. Then she poured herself a glass of wine and started upstairs. Halfway up, she must have felt ill or weak. She stopped, sat down, and carefully put the glass down on the step above. That afternoon, John Pinnie came into the house and found her lying there, dead of a heart attack.

A small private service was held at Steepletop several days later, attended by a few close friends. Norma read "The Poet and His Book." Allan Ross Macdougall read "Dirge Without Music." Then Esther Adams played Beethoven's "Appassionata," which Edna had especially loved. From music and poetry, the two ramparts of her life, came these last eloquent salutes to Edna St. Vincent Millay.

Selected Bibliography

By Edna St. Vincent Millay:

The following list contains the principal works in order of first appearance. With the exception of the article "Fear," all the items were eventually published under the imprint of Harper & Brothers, New York.

Renascence and Other Poems. 1917.
Aria da Capo. 1920.
A Few Figs from Thistles. 1920. New poems were added in subsequent editions; final version, 1922.
The Lamp and the Bell. 1921.
Second April. 1921.
Two Slatterns and a King. 1921.
The Harp-Weaver and Other Poems. 1923.
Distressing Dialogues. 1924. (Under the pseudonym Nancy Boyd.)
The King's Henchman. 1927.
"Fear," *Outlook*, November 9, 1927.
The Buck in the Snow. 1928.
Poems Selected for Young People. 1929.
Fatal Interview. 1931.
The Princess Marries the Page. 1932.
Wine from These Grapes. 1934.
Flowers of Evil. From the French of Charles Baudelaire, with George Dillon, 1936.
Conversation at Midnight. 1937.
Huntsman, What Quarry? 1939.

257

Make Bright the Arrows. 1940.
Invocation to the Muses. 1941.
Collected Sonnets. 1941.
The Murder of Lidice. 1942.
Collected Lyrics. 1943.
Poem and Prayer for an Invading Army. 1944.
Letters of Edna St. Vincent Millay, edited by Allan Ross
  Macdougall. 1952.
Mine the Harvest. 1954.
Collected Poems. 1956.

Individual poems and letters not contained in any of the collections above, but from which excerpts have been quoted:

First poem. In Elizabeth Breuer, "Mother of Poets," *Pictorial
  Review*, March 1930, p. 6.
"Dishpan Song." *Ibid.*
Verse beginning "Let me not shout into the world's great
  ear." Karl Yost, *A Bibliography of the Works of Edna
  St. Vincent Millay*, p. 60.
"The Patient Periodical." *Vassar Miscellany Weekly*, May
  12, 1916, pp. 1 and 5.
Lines from last notebook. Vincent Sheean, *The Indigo Bunt-
  ing*, p. 32.
Letter to New York *World*, October 6, 1927, p. 12. Re-
  printed in Yost, pp. 64–65.
Letters to Charlotte Babcock Sills, October 12, 1917, and
  December 1917. Vassar Collection.

About Edna St. Vincent Millay:

Most of the existing material on Millay is scattered through
a large number of articles, reviews, memoirs, newspaper accounts, and books which often contain only brief, though
useful, sections about her. The following is a partial listing
of the principal items used in preparing this volume. An

extensive bibliographic file is to be found at the Vassar College Library. Yost is invaluable for the earlier years.

Adams, Franklin P. *The Diary of Our Own Samuel Pepys*, 2 vols. New York: Simon and Schuster, 1935.

Atkins, Elizabeth. *Edna St. Vincent Millay and Her Times*. Chicago: The University of Chicago Press, 1936.

Beatty, Jerome. " 'Best Sellers' in Verse," *The American Magazine*, January 1932, pp. 37, 102–106.

Bogan, Louise. *Achievement in American Poetry, 1900–1950*. Chicago: Henry Regnery Company, 1951.

————. *Selected Criticism*. New York: The Noonday Press, 1955.

Breuer, Elizabeth. "Edna St. Vincent Millay," *Pictorial Review*, November 1931, p. 2.

————. "Mother of Poets," *Pictorial Review*, March 1930, p. 6.

Bynner, Witter. "Edna St. Vincent Millay," *New Republic*, December 10, 1924, pp. 14–15.

Carpenter, Margaret Haley. *Sara Teasdale*. New York: The Schulte Publishing Company, 1960.

Chubb, Thomas Caldecot. "Shelley Grown Old," *North American Review*, Spring 1938, pp. 170–180.

Churchill, Allen. *The Improper Bohemians*. New York: E. P. Dutton & Company, 1959.

Cowley, Malcolm, ed. *After the Genteel Tradition*. New York: W. W. Norton & Co., 1937. (See especially Hildegarde Flanner, "Two Poets: Jeffers and Millay," pp. 155–167.)

————. *Exile's Return*. New York: The Viking Press, 1951.

Dell, Floyd. "Edna Millay Finds a Cook," New York *Herald Tribune Magazine*, March 19, 1933, p. 4.

————. "Edna St. Vincent Millay," *ibid.*, May 3, 1931, p. 3.

————. *Homecoming*. New York: Farrar & Rinehart, 1933.

————. "Not Roses, Roses All the Way." Unpublished ms.

————. "The Rise of Greenwich Village," *Love in Greenwich Village*. New York: George H. Doran, 1926, pp. 13–44.

Deutsch, Babette. *This Modern Poetry*. New York: W. W. Norton & Co., 1935.

Deutsch, Helen; Hanau, Stella. *The Provincetown*. New York: Farrar & Rinehart, 1931.

Eastman, Max. *Great Companions*. New York: Farrar, Straus and Cudahy, 1959.

————. "A Passing Fashion," *The Nation*, December 5, 1928, pp. 628–630.

————. "Sweet Disease of Otherness," *American Mercury*, May 1952, pp. 107–109.

Estes, Richard D. "The 'Vincent' Camden Knew," *Yankee*, September 1953, pp. 19–23.

Fisher, Ethel Knight. "Edna St. Vincent Millay's Youth," *St. Nicholas*, September 1936, pp. 48–49, and October 1936, p. 52.

Gregory, Horace; Zaturenska, Marya. *A History of American Poetry 1900–1940*. New York: Harcourt, Brace and Co., 1946.

Hackett, Francis. "Edna St. Vincent Millay," *New Republic*, December 24, 1956, pp. 21–22.

Haight, Elizabeth Hazelton. "Vincent at Steepletop," *Vassar Alumnae Magazine*, February 1957, pp. 11–14.

————. "Vincent at Vassar," *Vassar Alumnae Magazine*, May 1951, pp. 14–20.

Hillyer, Robert. "Of Her Essential Heart and Spirit," *The New York Times Book Review*, April 25, 1954, p. 5.

Humphries, Rolfe. "Edna St. Vincent Millay: 1892–1950," *The Nation*, December 30, 1950, p. 704.

Jenney, Florence G. "As I Remember Her," *Russell Sage College Alumnae Quarterly*, Winter 1951, pp. 8–9.

Joughin, G. Louis; Morgan, Edmund M. *The Legacy of Sacco and Vanzetti*. New York: Harcourt, Brace and Co., 1948.

King, Grace Hamilton. *The Development of the Social Consciousness of Edna St. Vincent Millay as Manifested in Her Poetry*. Unpublished doctoral dissertation, New York University, 1943.

Kirkland, Winifred and Frances. *Girls Who Became Writers*. New York: Harper & Brothers, 1933.

Kreymborg, Alfred. *Our Singing Strength*. New York: Coward-McCann, Inc., 1929.

Langner, Lawrence. *The Magic Curtain*. New York: E. P. Dutton & Company, 1951.

Loggins, Vernon. *I Hear America*. New York: Thomas Y. Crowell Company, 1937.

MacCracken, Henry Noble. *The Hickory Limb*. New York: Charles Scribner's Sons, 1950.

Macdougall, Allan Ross. "Husband of a Genius," *Delineator*, October 1934, p. 21.

Millett, Fred B. *Contemporary American Authors*. New York: Harcourt, Brace and Co., 1940.

"Miss Millay, Poet on a Farm," *House & Garden*, November 1942, pp. 40–41.

Monroe, Harriet. *A Poet's Life*. New York: The Macmillan Company, 1938.

Powys, Llewelyn. *The Verdict of Bridlegoose*. New York: Harcourt, Brace and Co., 1926.

―――. *The Letters of Llewelyn Powys*, ed. by Louis Wilkinson. London: John Lane The Bodley Head, 1943.

"Radio, War, Poetry," *The New York Times*, October 18, 1942, VIII:10.

Ransom, John Crowe. "The Poet as Woman," *The World's Body*. New York: Charles Scribner's Sons, 1938, pp. 76–110.

Rittenhouse, Jessie B. *My House of Life*. Boston: Houghton Mifflin Company, 1934.

Sheean, Vincent. *The Indigo Bunting*. New York: Harper & Brothers, 1951.

Sills, Charlotte Babcock. Letter to the Editor, *Vassar Alumnae Magazine*, December 1960, pp. 25–26.

Simpson, Dorothy. *The Maine Islands*. Philadelphia: J. B. Lippincott Company, 1960.

Taber, Gladys. "Poet's Kitchen," *Ladies' Home Journal*, February 1949, pp. 55–56, 183–185.

Taggard, Genevieve. "A Woman's Anatomy of Love," *New York Herald Tribune Books*, April 19, 1931, p. 3.

Tate, Allen. *Reactionary Essays on Poetry and Ideas*. New York: Charles Scribner's Sons, 1936.

Taylor, Deems. "Edna St. Vincent Millay 1892–1950," *Commemorative Tributes of the American Academy of Arts and Letters, 1942–1951*, New York, 1951, pp. 103–108.

Van Doren, Carl. *Three Worlds*. New York: Harper & Brothers, 1936.

Ware, Caroline F. *Greenwich Village 1920–1930*. Boston: Houghton Mifflin Company, 1935.

Wilson, Edmund. *The Shores of Light*. New York: Farrar, Straus and Young, 1952. (See especially "Epilogue, 1952: Edna St. Vincent Millay," pp. 744–793.)

Yost, Karl. *A Bibliography of the Works of Edna St. Vincent Millay*, with an Essay in Appreciation by Harold Lewis Cook. New York: Harper & Brothers, 1937.

A useful group of newspaper clippings about Edna St. Vincent Millay can be seen in Room 315 T (Theatre Collection) of the New York Public Library. Among the good periodical sources are the following student publications of Vassar College (also available at the New York Public Library):

Vassar Miscellany: March 12, 1915.

Vassar Miscellany Monthly: December 1916, May 1917.

Vassar Miscellany Weekly: March 17, 1916, May 5, 1916, May 12, 1916, December 15, 1916.

Vassar Miscellany News: May 19, 1917, January 16, 1924, November 28, 1928, June 12, 1929, November 11, 1950, November 19, 1952, November 5, 1958, November 12, 1958.

Index

About the Author

Miriam Gurko has written numerous magazine articles on a variety of subjects. Her background of research and editorial work for academic and scholarly organizations was useful training for the large amount of research necessary for *The Lives and Times of Peter Cooper* and *Restless Spirit: The Life of Edna St. Vincent Millay*.

Mrs. Gurko was born in Union City, New Jersey, graduated from the University of Wisconsin, and now lives in New York City with her husband, a professor of English, and their two children.